Creature Needs

CREATURE NEEDS

—

WRITERS RESPOND TO THE SCIENCE
OF ANIMAL CONSERVATION

Christopher Kondrich, Lucy Spelman,
and Susan Tacent, Editors

University of Minnesota Press
Minneapolis
London

Illustrations by Franco Zacha

Published by the University of Minnesota Press
111 Third Avenue South, Suite 290
Minneapolis, MN 55401-2520
http://www.upress.umn.edu

ISBN 978-1-5179-1831-6 (pb)

A Cataloging-in-Publication record for this book is available
from the Library of Congress.

Printed in the United States of America on acid-free paper

The University of Minnesota is an equal-opportunity
educator and employer.

32 31 30 29 28 27 26 25 24   10 9 8 7 6 5 4 3 2 1

This book emerged from the work of Creature Conserve, a 501(c)(3) nonprofit outreach organization dedicated to bringing together artists, designers, writers, and experts with scientific and traditional knowledge together in a supportive, welcoming space to learn about threats to wildlife, share empathy for animals, exchange ideas, and find opportunities for growth at the intersection of art, science, and conservation.

Contents

AIR
—
13

FOOD
—
59

WATER
—
93

New Arts of Conservation

—

LUCY SPELMAN

I want to know what it's like to be a beetle or a giraffe or a frigate bird; how it feels to fly or use a tail for balance or navigate using a magnetic field. I could go on. My love of animals stems from a deep curiosity about them. I am all smiles in their presence. I also feel intensely responsible for their well-being. I wake up each day wondering if the animals are okay, the result, at least in part, of a jarring childhood memory: a polar bear with green fur (from algae overgrowth) pacing in a small cage in New York City with car horns going off all around it and no trees, let alone snow, in sight.

If an animal is sick, injured, or distressed because of something my species has done, then I see it as our (human) responsibility to fix it. If we have confined an animal or limited it in such a way that it cannot live out its life naturally, then it is up to us, at a bare minimum, to meet its basic needs for air, food, water, shelter, room to move, and each other. The setting does not matter. There is no part of this earth left untouched by humans. It could be a bumblebee in someone's yard searching for pollen in a sea of green grass, a trio of Asian elephants in a zoo standing all winter on a cold cement floor, or a family of giant river otters in Guyana moving their newborn cubs from one den to another to protect them from poachers.

As a zoological medicine specialist, I do what I can to take responsibility. I treat animals of all kinds, aquatic and terrestrial, with and without a backbone, anywhere I can. I share what I know through my writing and teaching. I learn from colleagues and look for opportunities to lead: I ran the Smithsonian's National Zoo in Washington, D.C., for five years and the Mountain Gorilla Veterinary Project in Rwanda for three. I am currently a senior lecturer at the Rhode Island School of Design, a consultant for National Geographic Kids Books, an exotics specialist at Ocean State Veterinary Specialists, and executive director of Creature Conserve, the nonprofit I founded in 2015.

I am not alone. We—scientists who work in wildlife conservation— are a subset of hundreds of thousands of people from all walks of life, a mix of citizens, professionals, and politicians all over the world who have dedicated their lives to saving species and their habitats. We have had some successes. American Alligators, Giant Pandas, Humpback Whales, and Peregrine Falcons are no longer on the brink of extinction. New genetic engineering techniques will soon re-create (most of) the Passenger Pigeon and Darwin's Frog. But we are not doing enough.

Animals that were extremely rare when I began my career are even rarer (Sumatran Tiger) or extinct (Northern White Rhinoceros). Species we thought were plentiful (African Lion) are now in trouble. We continue to degrade our natural resources, cutting rain forests, dynamiting coral reefs, and burning fossil fuels. We hunt, fish, and trade animal pieces and parts until entire species are gone. We grow crops in monoculture until we exhaust the soil. We have eight billion people on earth compared to two billion when I was born. The result is that we are losing species at an alarming rate.

Some may say the loss of biodiversity is no problem; that our technology will get us through. Our life experience tells us otherwise: drought, famine, extreme weather, pandemic, and invasive species. Conservation (verb: to balance our needs with those of the rest of nature) is failing. We are not inclusive enough; we need more disciplines; we need to combine all ways of knowing—science, art, traditional ecological knowledge—to make informed decisions. We need to be more just. And we need to spend a lot more money.

What we are doing is not working.

Another animal encounter seared in my memory is the day I sat watching a baby mountain gorilla rubbing her runny nose. She was fighting a respiratory infection that we knew could be fatal for her and others in her family group. Her mother was coughing. I was very worried about losing this infant. It had happened before. At the time we had not yet proven that we were part of the problem. Everyone who visits the gorillas (including, ironically, myself and those of us charged with their protection) brings their diseases with them. But deep down I knew it.

I heard a car go by, then drumming, then a human baby crying. I could smell smoke from a cooking fire. I hiked back down the mountain thinking, *How is it that I feel responsible for the health of an entire species when in fact this is a shared duty?* We are all stewards of nature and her creatures. All children grow up loving their stuffed animals and book or video characters. This emotion is still there. We just have to tap into it.

The only way to change course is to rapidly increase the number of people engaged in wildlife conservation. This is our greatest challenge: few of us consider ourselves conservationists, even though we are indeed taking informed action, whether recycling or planting for pollinators or saving energy at home. The information is out there—on the internet, in books, and in journal articles—but it is meaningless without connection, both to nature and to each other.

The baby gorilla improved each day over the next week. Thankfully, we did not need to intervene as we would during the next outbreak. For me, watching her that day was one of those life-changing moments: I decided to work differently. It was time for me to take my years of experience and knowledge of science and put them in a new place.

How do we make an activity that has historically been top-down, elitist, and polarizing into something that we all do and we know we are doing it, together? What will motivate us to change our ways? I believe the arts informed, inspired, and prompted by science have the power to direct our attention to the ongoing loss of species and what we can do about it.

Art taps into our emotions and our subconscious. It reminds us that all life is connected; we are animals, too. It deepens our understanding of this interdependency and helps us explore how we feel about animals and our relationships with them. It creates context (cultural, historical, social, political) and space for our conversations about wildlife conservation.

It makes the scientific and traditional knowledge we use to make decisions more accessible, meaningful, and real, and the solutions more actionable. It generates imaginary worlds that draw us closer to nature and our inherent love of animals.

Art is also far more likely to inspire a change in our behavior than a string of scientific facts. As you will see in the writings that follow, when we bring artists, writers, and scientists together to explore the human connection to nature, we can and do create pathways to a healthier world for all species, including ours.

What Humans Owe Animals

—

CHRISTOPHER KONDRICH

Today, new forms of animal cruelty turn up all the time—
without even being recognized as cruelty, since their
impact on the lives of intelligent beings is barely consid-
ered. So, we have not just the overdue debt of the past, but
a new moral debt that has increased a thousandfold and is
continuously increasing.

—Martha Nussbaum

Although this quotation from Martha Nussbaum, renowned philosopher and the Ernst Freund Distinguished Service Professor of Law and Ethics at the University of Chicago, appears in her book *Justice for Animals: Our Collective Responsibility,* it was included in an excerpt published by *Time* magazine under the headline "What Humans Owe Animals." The headline is notable. There is a moral clarity to it, a directness that is both startling and refreshing. It could certainly have been posed as a question—asking readers whether humans owe animals anything, or whether animals can even be considered creatures to which something can be owed.

The headline, like Nussbaum's argument, invites readers to consider animals as deserving of what has been taken from them: their habitats, surely, but more to the point, their livelihoods, their society, their *agency.* "Animals do need relief from pain," Nussbaum writes, "but they also need . . . the chance to be the makers of their own lives." This notion of agency gets to the heart of what we—as we learn more, and in greater depth, about the lives of animals, as well as in this time that we've come to call the Anthropocene—owe them. When there is no aspect of animal life that is untouched by human actions (whether directly or indirectly, on purpose or by accident), they do not have the kind of agency they deserve, and the ways in which agency is withheld from them, the ways in which they are kept from being "the makers of their own lives," as Nussbaum writes, is myriad. In addition to habitat destruction, what immediately comes to mind is factory farming, poaching, and game hunting. But human cruelty also comes in the form of noise and light pollution, pesticide use, damming, drought, declines in prey populations, and disruptions of migratory patterns. Even well-meaning attempts to save or reintroduce one species can have negative impacts on others. And so much of this happens without many of us noticing it.

But scientists have noticed, are noticing—this is what they do. Every day new articles are published in science journals that further illuminate the implications and consequences of human cruelties. What conservation scientists show us with every study, every analysis, every conclusion, is that other species have needs, that these needs are interdependent and overlapping, and that they are being ignored in favor of our own. However, conservation science also shows us that we have the knowledge required to ensure that the needs of all species are being met—we just have to exert our agency, which, of course, requires the social, political, and, indeed, moral will to do so.

This is where the arts come in. What conservation science provides writers with gets at the heart of what a writer must do: make the real *feel* real to readers. Make a number, a statistic, an assessment, a theory, feel embodied, storied. Make *information* into *knowledge* (the kind that is "proved upon our pulses," as Keats once wrote) and maybe even *truth*. If what scientists, through research and analysis, reveal to us are facts and their interpretation of them—what can be measured, observed, verified—then, perhaps, one way of considering what writers do is distilling the facts of the world into truth, the kind of truth that stirs us, moves us, stays with us long after the poem, story, or essay is over. Truth is the realm where facts take on meaning beyond what exactly they state, and so it is the realm of literature. For poets and writers, truth from facts can be conjured, evoked, implied, discovered, brought to the fore through juxtaposition, which is to say, by doing what the poets and writers included in *Creature Needs: Writers Respond to the Science of Animal Conservation* have done in ways that reveal what is at stake when we leave the facts unheeded.

But this is not to say that there is only one truth, or one definitive truth, that the facts of a particular article leads a writer to derive. Nor is there a sole means of deriving it. The works in this collection offer inspired ways of deriving truth from facts, giving readers various interpretations of what it means to write in conversation with another piece of writing—how explicit to make the exchange or convergence of ideas, whether to write in response to specific or overall findings, whether to borrow language or hybridize form, et cetera. Thalia Field's "Jump/Scare" and Sofia Samatar's "The Sublime Is a Foreign Species," for example, in starting with a list of keywords, borrow from the conventions of science scholarship to explore how our cultural understanding and knowledge about animal precarity is obtained and deployed. Ramona Ausubel's "Home Range" and Sharma Shields's "Keystone Species," meanwhile, want to fold the facts about animal precarity into stories about the precarity of human life and the losses and traumas that make us want to find solace in the more-than-human world.

While science requires a precise, specific question to be explored through field study, the synthesis of data, and so on, the conceptual scope of literature is impossible to delineate (or anticipate), and so, in the hands of so many poets and writers in this collection, political, historical, cultural, spiritual, and experiential knowledge get added to the kind of knowledge that science provides. In "Words at Dawn Break," Beth Piatote recasts the noise pollution that is the cause of the changing syntax of birdsong as "colonization" that "disrupts the animal chorus" and "disorders the dawn." These lines give the impact of incessant and intrusive human-made decibels social, political, and historical knowledge, mapping what, in *The Nutmeg's Curse,* Amitav Ghosh calls "the rhetoric and imagery of empire" onto that which is supposed to exist empireless. Craig Santos Perez's "Three Sonnets without a Barrier Reef," meanwhile, provides generational and familial knowledge, the kind of knowledge that stems from fear born out of love, the fear of what the world will hold for those we love the most. In the second sonnet, the speaker is reading his daughter a book called *The Great Barrier Reef* while knowing about the reef's consistent decline: "She loves every colorful picture / of tropical fish and intricate corals; I love / that the pictures never change." Because the sonnets are also providing us with information drawn from the article that inspired it, these lines are freighted with the knowledge of what is happening off the page, as well as with a sense of loss, worry, and regret the speaker is experiencing. The implied irony of this moment in Santos Perez's poem adds to the knowledge that the science provides by reflecting back to readers the complexities of how we currently live— juggling dread and dissonance, hope and hopes dashed by inaction in equal measure.

The diversity of approaches and aesthetics across *Creature Needs* reveals not just the imaginative strength of contemporary poets and writers but also the power and urgency of writing from science. We simply no longer live in a world in which poems and stories about the so-called *natural world* (a term that reifies our feelings of separateness from it) will suffice. This is not to say that we must jettison the wonder beyond words that, say, a forest of songbirds instills in us, but literature that aspires to *speak to the moment* must no longer neglect the science that articulates the problems, as well as the solutions, to the decline of this forest of songbirds. We need to be able to behold, in poetry and prose, the wonder of the living world while also having the humility to behold the shadow of human cruelties we have cast with equal vividness, lyricism, and clarity. We need science-informed literature in order to write work that *speaks to the moment so that we might rectify the problems the moment entails.* This is the gift that every contributor in this book has given us.

Six Basic Needs

—

SUSAN TACENT

I grew up in urban Brooklyn, New York. The wildlife I experienced on my block of brick rowhouses was a smattering of squirrels, pigeons, and maple trees planted into two-foot by three-foot cement-delineated squares, every twelve feet or so. Probably a robin or two.

I currently live in suburban Rhode Island, where from my windows, on any given day, in addition to squirrels and doves (those near cousins of my city pigeon), I listen to the violining crickets and sizzle of bees. Depending on the time of the year, I watch broods of pecking turkeys, cawing crows, chirping cardinals, squawking blue jays, chittering chipmunks, and what my sound identifier identifies as tufted titmice, Carolina wrens, catbirds, flickers, downy woodpeckers, and, yes, robins. At night, the screech owl warbles. Occasionally, a Cooper's hawk, a red fox, or a slinky coyote dashes by, and I've learned not to watch as predator and prey remind me that those nature shows I watched somewhat fearfully as a kid were real. A mama bunny nested her six babies right in the middle of my exuberant patch of thyme. Once, a monarch butterfly bumped my right ear on its way from somewhere to somewhere else. Once a half-grown deer galloped by.

I make an effort to be a good neighbor to them. I scrub the birdbaths and keep them filled with cool fresh water. I fill the feeders with reasonable amounts of appropriate seed. I watch them nibble and bathe, listen to them scold and invite, grateful we share a neighborhood. I plant perennials for the pollinators and gleefully watch them go to seed.

Though I've learned to be satisfied with this much interaction, my gut tells me to do more. I want to keep the feeders filled day and night and in all seasons, but I've learned that if I do so, I risk inviting avian illnesses in species that would never feed so incessantly or in such close proximity to one another. I want to put out blankets and raw meat for the coyote, but I've learned that if the coyote becomes too comfortable with me, other human–coyote interactions may not go so well. I want to scoop up the mama bunny and her six lovely babies and bring them inside when it's stormy outside. I want to stand in the busy street that runs by my house and force every car to detour or at the very least slow the hell down. The anxiety I can produce in myself by worrying about every creature who happens to live in close proximity to me or passes by isn't healthy—for me or for them. More importantly, it isn't helpful.

Much of my knowledge about interacting with nonhuman species comes from my interaction with Dr. Lucy Spelman. Lucy and I have been friends for decades. This friendship is based in large part on a shared love for the so-called natural world and a fierce desire to make things better for all species. When she founded Creature Conserve in 2015, I was there from the beginning, giving whatever support I could for the birth of an organization with the potential to bring needed understanding, and therefore change, to the world.

Education—sharing one's knowledge and training with others—is one of the cornerstones of Creature Conserve. Science, with its investment in hypothesis, research, and analysis, is another. And so is Creativity—the imagination-driven expression of the actual and the possible. Over the years, I have cotaught Creature Conserve workshops and attended Creature Conserve lectures. In my teaching for the organization, I share what I have learned about the process of science-informed art and generating new work with writers and poets. With every iteration of these workshops, I become more confident in the critical and timely importance of the process.

All living creatures—bird, bat, human, snail, alewife, moth, dolphin, dragonfly, elephant, cheetah, and so on—share the same six basic needs: air, food, water, shelter, room to move, and each other. These needs form the organizational framework of this book.

To fill this framework, my coeditor poet Christopher Kondrich and I invited writers and poets to choose one of these six needs. We were moved and gratified by how quickly the yeses came back, often the same day, sometimes within the hour of our hitting *send*. The extremely small percentage of those who said no did so with regret and great enthusiasm for the project.

To those who said yes, we sent an open-source, peer-reviewed scientific article chosen by Lucy and published in the last few years. Each article covered a different species living in the United States whose health and existence is threatened by anthropogenic activity—that is, the activities of human animals. The article became the prompt, and the only limit we set was 3,000 words or ten pages of new, previously unpublished work. They sent their responses to us, and it was thrilling to see where the science had taken them and where they had taken the science. Every response felt necessary and urgent, like a gift we didn't know we needed until we held it in our hands.

Excerpts from each scientific article precede each response. The book may be read cover to cover. Or, you may choose to read the science first, and if you do, we hope you'll consider writing your own response before reading the one in the book. Or maybe you'll read one response at a time from each of the six sections, going back to the entries in that order. Or perhaps birds first, then mammals, then fish.

In a way, this book serves as a map, one that locates our place among other animals insofar as their needs and ours are the same. And it is a map of the interconnectedness of the six needs. What good is clean air if the water is polluted? What good is room to move if a fragmented habitat keeps creatures apart?

The book as a whole provides a cross-disciplinary overview of the challenges and rewards of active conservation in the United States. We focused on species living in the United States as a necessary constraint and a good place to start. But of course all living creatures worldwide share the same six basic needs.

Air, food, water, shelter, room to move, and each other.

Each—and every—other.

Side-Blotched Lizard *(Uta stansburiana)*

AIR

—

All life on Earth evolved over the last four billion years under a specific set of conditions, including those of our atmosphere. To make the energy needed to run their cellular machinery, animals use oxygen, plants require carbon dioxide and sunlight, and symbionts such as coral need all three. Oxygen and carbon dioxide, along with nitrogen and water, are contained in our troposphere, a miles-thick layer of air that overlies the land and water. The moisture in the troposphere generates our weather patterns, and the ozone layer above it filters out the strongest rays from the sun. The gas and water molecules together scatter the light to create our blue skies.

In many ways, the air we breathe is beautifully simple. But how we get oxygen out of the air and into our cells is not. Animals do this by diffusion. In the simplest creatures, no organized structure is needed for this process other than a cell membrane. The oxygen moves from regions of high concentration to low. In more complex organisms, diffusion happens across blood vessels organized in a cardiovascular system. Such organisms include animals with a backbone: the vertebrates.

Various structures facilitate diffusion in different vertebrate animals. Fish have gills, amphibians rely on their skin and a sac-like lung, reptiles and birds have both lungs and air sacs, and mammals possess lungs. These delicate structures are easily disrupted by alterations to the troposphere, including changing weather patterns, humidity, and temperature; by disruption of the ozone layer; and by airborne pollutants.

To use one example, canaries were used as sentinels for toxic gases (mostly carbon monoxide) that can build up in coal mines. Birds have incredibly efficient respiratory systems. Their air sacs act as bellows to move air into and through the lungs and then into another set of air sacs, a circuit that requires a two-breath sequence. The result is that air spends more time in the lungs. So, birds have twice the chance of taking in a toxin from the air. When the "canary in the coal mine" died, it was time for the human animals (the miners), with their less efficient respiratory system, to get out.

Air is also a medium in which terrestrial animals live. It transmits light and sound and, in addition to oxygen, naturally holds carbon dioxide, moisture, heat, pollen, and a tremendous variety of smells, some organic and others not. Animals use the air to find their way, sense their surroundings, communicate with each other, and detect danger.

—*Lucy Spelman*

Females of the glowworm *Lampyris noctiluca* produce long-lasting glows to attract flying males, and several field studies show that various types of artificial light at night (ALAN) decrease male attraction. Many lightning bug fireflies engage in flash dialogs in which females give flash responses to male courtship signals. ALAN has been shown to reduce courtship flashing by three lightning bug taxa: *Pteroptyx maipo, Photuris,* and male *Photinus.* Furthermore, *Photinus pyralis* females exposed to ALAN responded less often to male courtship signals and showed a nonsignificant reduction in mating success. Therefore, several lines of evidence indicate that ALAN interferes with firefly reproductive behavior and may heighten extinction risk.

FROM
"A Global Perspective on Firefly Extinction Threats"

BY
Sara M. Lewis, Choong Hay Wong, Avalon C. S. Owens,
Candace Fallon, Sarina Jepsen, et al.

PUBLISHED IN
BioScience 70, issue 2 (February 2020): 157–67

Fireflies

—

CHARLES BAXTER

For Lynne Raughley and Peter Ho Davies

In the children's fairy tale, the girl and boy—the bravest in the village—
escape from the burning house and flee into the woods, pursued by the
slime ogre with no face and three legs, a monster in the shape of a slug on
fire. It has no eyes, but it feels its way forward like a hungry bat.

The two brave children run deeper into the forest, and the trees regard
them impassively. The trees have seen such children before, running
away from witches and wizards, dragons, and men intent on being mur-
derers. The trees have seen it all, many times.

Night is falling. The three-legged ogre has given up and crawled back. But
now the children are very deep in the woods, and they are lost. There is
no path toward home. Like Hansel and Gretel, who left a trail of bread
crumbs that the birds ate, they do not know where they are.

In the children's fairy tale, at twilight, the fireflies begin to appear. Somehow the children know that the fireflies will lead them to safety. Each
firefly has a tiny light that appears briefly, now on, now off, like an airy
floating point of light. The light is beautiful, magical.

In the story, the fireflies are like guardian angels, and the tale ends when
the children are safe, led to the old woodcutter's cabin, where they each
have a bowl of porridge for dinner. The next morning, they find their way
to the village, where the mayor praises them.

They live happily ever after. The story is sentimental but memorable. When you first came to my house, we sat on the porch, and at twilight, the fireflies emerged from the woods, and their lights twinkled—a word I rarely use—and you said you'd never seen them before.

Like so much in our lives, they are endangered. So much seems to be passing away, including their flickering lights, visible that evening in Ann Arbor, Michigan. Their luminosity always gave me a heart-fluttering—those bright, tiny insect souls rising up.

On a national scale, an estimated 140,000–328,000 birds are killed annually by turbine collisions. Large soaring birds (e.g., storks, vultures, and eagles) in particular are at high risk of demographic consequences from fatalities at wind energy facilities due to their low reproductive rates and their reliance on topographic and weather conditions preferred by wind energy facility developers. Furthermore, a number of environmental, temporal, and behavioral factors may influence whether a soaring bird will fly above or within the rotor-swept zone of modern industrial horizontal-axis wind turbines.

FROM

"Flight Response to Spatial and Temporal Correlates
Informs Risk from Wind Turbines to the California Condor"

BY

Sharon A. Poessel, Joseph Brandt, Laura C. Mendenhall,
Melissa A. Braham, Michael J. Lanzone, et al.

PUBLISHED IN

The Condor 120, issue 2 (May 1, 2018): 330–42

Ishkode: Of Fires

—

KIMBERLY BLAESER

And in the foreground the fields were fixed in fire,
And the flames flowered in our flesh.
> —N. Scott Momaday, "The Burning"

i.
Agamiing. On the water.

Late in October, I lower myself, hatted and heavily-layered, into the kayak. I am tired of waiting for winds to calm and temperatures to give me one more warm day's reprieve in which to say goodbye. We are pushing the season, *dawaagin*. Ice will form soon. We have already had one snow.

So I make my way onto Farm Lake, along the rocky shores, and into the Kawishiwi River. I want to sit in the marsh with my morning coffee, tuck myself under the tree where I once watched the rapid head of a black-backed woodpecker. He reminded me with each determined hammer of his beak to seek the buried. I want to paddle nooks where river otters might pop up like jack-in-the-boxes—head up—head down, head up—head down, teasing me to follow. Farther along, I will recall *makwa*, the black bear swimming among autumn waters, crossing before me, shaking a rainbow into the air, then ambling into the woods lining shore. Gone like all apparitions. The water just there will always say *bear* now when I pass.

This is how we story ourselves with place. Each year I tuck the comfort of Minnesota's Northwoods and Boundary Waters Canoe Area Wilderness around me. Here I live in a world where I become small again in the immensity of this ecosystem. A cosmology of *nibi*. I might look up to find a bull moose, antlers still velveted with spring. Night after night, the depth of the stars swallow me. Loons call. Occasionally we hear wolves, their howl shivering along the marrow of our bones. Something, some way of being, sweeps clean our kingdom of I. Here we become rhythm of repeating waves, the slow spiral of hawks, fog dancing on morning lake.

In my kayak, I am nearly level with the tea-colored waters that hold copper, tannin, and history. On hot summer days, I prune my fingers while I swim, float; become the scent of northern waters. At night, my hair tells my pillow about lake weeds. My eyes whisper image—their closed lids a tracery of the sun glittering, the sun spilling geometric designs across the canvas of lake. We dream in new languages.

The daylight, too, reveals secrets. The black-capped chickadees come when I imitate their call. They flutter in, then perch on my shoulder, my foot, even my hopeful camera. Their tiny claws tickle my hand as they feed. One bite, two, a third for the road. The red squirrels warn and chase one another away, keep the peanut bounty I offer for themselves alone. The pine marten climbs into the bird feeder to eat, but watches warily and never stays long. We make friends with the creature's routines, and they with ours.

But chance encounters shimmer, moments out of time. Today, admitting I am cold despite my layers, I turn toward home. Just then I spot a flock, white against the dark clouds. They angle and turn, lift and glide— aerial revelers. I forget my icy hands. Two break formation, head my way. They are coming fast; I lift my camera just as they fly directly over me. Glorious eight-foot wingspan, thrusting necks longer than their whole bodies, and black legs that point back alongside their tail feathers. *Naabi-ziig.* Trumpeter swans.

Not the curving water beauty of fairytale, but an ephemeral creature of air, of *noodin.* Three small flaps then the glide. Airfoil wings barely moving. They soar over me, past me, then make a dramatic landing. I listen as they trumpet back and forth, swim a little one way and then another. Lucky for me, they change their minds. This is not where they want to be after all. With great pomp, they run along the water, their flap splash flap splash builds up lift until they can get their twentysome-pound bodies airborne. They rise and turn, make one more pass by me, before arrowing out of sight.

Both spent and exhilarated, I practice my own movement ecology, make the most of each stroke, catch the wind when I can. I have seen swans in water lift a wing like a sail and let the breeze carry them. Adaptation their strength more than ours. Obligate soaring birds use air. Heavy, they need and learn to mine the uplifts, conserve energy spent in flapping.

I spend too much of my life flapping. Today I promise a small devotion to bird ecology, to air currents and strategic resting movement.

For this was the not-quite post-pandemic summer of drought. Of fires and the memory of fires. The parceled threat of a burning planet.

How shall we sing the planet in all its intimate beauty—in the midst of its destruction? Is writing place, writing our ancient belonging, now inevitably elegy? How spend ourselves for repair?

ii.
Mikwendagwad. A journal of fire.

Monday, August 16
Above us, the sky swims through the changing pallet of sunrise as we step onto the dock at six to cross the lake. Amber flies out of Duluth this morning. Summer starts its endings.

Quiet fills the car on the drive back. But the six-block main street of Two Harbors has recently sprouted Back Forty Books. We cheer ourselves with browsing, chat with the owner while paying. When I mention our water-access cabin outside of Ely, he says his wife has just called to alert him about a fire on Highway 2—our route home. We abandon our other chores and set off on the first leg of 2, a corridor of highway in the Superior National Forest. No sign of smoke. The road jogs after twenty-five miles. Sure enough. At the jog, the road is closed. A patrolwoman stationed there suggests an alternate route, which takes us 75 miles out of our way.

As Len drives, I google. Begin obsessively tracking the spread of what will become known as the Greenwood Fire. We arrive after sunset at our dock, cross the water. *Agaami-zaaga'igan,* on the other side of the lake, we feel safe.

Tuesday, August 17

Morning. The fire has spread to 1,000 acres. Minnesota National Guard called in. Evacuations started. Evening, 2,000 acres.

In between tracking the fire, I work then ask myself how I can keep on working when everything is aflame. A voice thirty years gone asks, *What can we do when we can do nothing?* My mother's lament when the DOE planned to store high-level nuclear waste on White Earth lands. The disenfranchised feeling precisely the level of powerlessness planned.

Today, those who would burn our future for oil profits and industry hold more power than those who would protect it. But maybe the winds are shifting.

Wednesday, August 18

Morning on the ledge rock. Planes just flew over. On their way to the fire? 3,200 acres now. Yes. It turns out they are fire bombers. Six planes scoop water from Sand Lake and drop it on the burning forest.

I imagine the planes' careful dives to the lake, their sky ballet. Under less dire circumstances, the waterfall spilling from the sky would be another wonder to watch.

Later, we paddle evening waters. Spot several eagles who spot us back. They fix us with sharp deep-set eyes before lifting off their perch. Their flap flap audible. Then they glide, lift on air drafts we cannot see— *abracadabra,* and recede into Boundary Waters' skies. *Migizi nindodem,* these clan relatives.

We cross paths with a loon and her chick. She dives, leaving only bubbles. Surfaces a few feet away a minnow in her mouth. We watch the hungry chick receive it. All this on repeat. Another minnow. A small rusty crayfish. Some hard-shelled insect.

A family of swans emerges out of the reeds, their necks straight as chair backs. Parents bookend the cygnets and the group of six moves through the water like an accomplished chorus line, turning in unison.

Geese, beaver and their dramatic tail splash—the normal, which is to say all the reasons we need the BWCA.

Only one missing element. We paddle back expecting a sky painting itself into night. Instead, haze. Smoke has stopped the sunset.

Thursday, August 19

A little stiff from paddling, we tumble into chairs early, sit outside, making our damp hello to morning. We eat, play cards, say goodbye to Josh. Len takes him across the lake. He leaves while other roads are still open.

4,285 acres and no containment. Fire crews from across the nation arrive. Google says lightning started the fire. But what caused the drought that left this forest and the burning acres in Arizona, California, Oregon, and Colorado vulnerable? Has Wisconsin's former governor gotten a foothold in the web and, there too, banned words like *climate change?*

The winds are strong and smoke has reached us. We cannot discern dusk amid the miasma of fire.

Friday, August 20

At 3 a.m. I wake Len. Smoke so thick, I think the fire is outside the cabin. We recon. No visible fire. Because the wind died down, the heavy smoke has settled around us, an ashy blanket. We wait for the promised rain, hoping it will aid fire crews.

Full morning and the air is better. I settle on the ledge rock with a manuscript I have promised to read.

Fire news continues bad: rain petered out before it reached us up north; the fire has jumped Highway 2. More residents are warned to evacuate. The evacuations move closer to us. We now have an alert on our phone. The Forest Service is canceling permits and closing the entire BWCA for the first time since the 1970s.

Saturday, August 21

9,062 acres. We receive "be prepared to evacuate" notices. Kevin, a peninsula neighbor, stops by. We debate. Begin watering the area around our cabin now with water pulled from the lake. Trees killed by spruce budworm would provide too much fuel if the Greenwood Fire reaches us.

Len is scheduled to leave tomorrow for travel. We debate that, too.

By day's end the fire has not spread and the forecast promises cooler, damper weather. Our "prepare to evacuate" notice is canceled.

Len packs. Kevin promises him that if they leave, I will leave, too.

Sunday, August 22

Beautiful boundary water's air this morning. Camp damp and bursting with fresh scents. *Minomaagwad.* Pine, cedar, spruce—some elixir of woods and northern waters. No smoke hanging over the lake. Air filled with birdsong and the chirps of chipmunks and squirrels.

Len leaves. I sit on the ledge rock with my work. I sit by the water and read, take calls, dream.

I let the world soothe me again:

> Just now the water looks like wide-wale corduroy—its movement
>   a caress.
> Sun, a peach swirl above the tree lines; lake, a swallowing silence.
> I watch where one white boat crosses . . . the line a yoga stretch for
>   my psyche.

Monday, August 23

Dimensions have disappeared. Lake and sky, indistinguishable. Their uniform silk gray, a womb around me.

Pace of work also dislocates me. I meet a deadline, fall into bed.

At 4 a.m. the reprieve ends.

In the campfire of night, smoke wakes me. Sore throat, crusted eyes. Nothing to do but wait. I close the window as if air were not on both sides.

Tuesday, August 24

Fire doubled in size in 24 hours. 30.5 square miles a-torch. 300 evacuations. News story quotes the fire commander who says the Greenwood Fire is "moving like a freight train." (Fire fear also spreading in my body.)

I think of charred forests, destroyed habitats. Our burning earth, the sixth extinction. Perhaps I will write loss by losing the round song of vowels: "sxth xtnctn." But who will read, heed this message?

If language is a mapping, the conquered have no hand in it. Language becomes propaganda, political—a danger. But only if the "masses" remain silent. Only if the cartography of story fails to hold natural spaces sacred.

Wednesday, August 25

A tactical burn is started on Hwy 1 to form a fire barrier.

A tactical retreat for me. My eyes, throat, heart cannot remain here. Tomorrow I go to my first in-person poetry event in seventeen months. At an art gallery. Miles from the smoke haze and air quality alerts. Metaphorical miles from the nitty gritty of statistics about containment (still zero), on reports of burned structures (12 so far), on the endless late-night premonitions.

But I cannot leave awareness at the base of gone trees, like a burnt offering; and wait for rescue. Truth is like air—we cannot lock it out. Everywhere we travel, it surrounds us.

iii.
Giwaanitoomin. Loss.

In the Arrowhead Region of Minnesota, a wildfire burned 26,797 acres or 42 square miles of prime habitat for wildlife, prime refuge for human life. Among the causes, Wikipedia mentions "exceptional drought intensity."

iv.
Gida-nanaa'itoomin. Repair.

Heavy with grief, the burden of "alternative facts," and anthropogenic misjudgment, we can still mine the currents, where each truth spoken lifts our voice on new airways.

Speak in song. Write in ash.

By 2050, wind is projected to account for 35% of all energy produced in the United States, resulting in 109,300 km^2 of land use across all 50 states. Despite this rapid and widespread development, surprisingly little is known about how wind farms affect surrounding ecosystems, especially fragile desert communities where much of this development will be concentrated. Most of the research investigating ecological effects of wind energy has focused on the direct impacts of wind turbines on bird and bat mortality. However, wind turbine development also alters a suite of habitat characteristics on the ground and imposes novel environmental disturbances that could increase physiological demands on nonvolant taxa. For populations of terrestrial species [like the side-blotched lizard] with small home ranges and limited dispersal abilities, alterations to the proximate landscape can be detrimental.

FROM

"Ectoparasite Load Is Reduced in Side-blotched Lizards *(Uta stansburiana)* at Wind Farms: Implications for Oxidative Stress"

BY

Valentina J. Alaasam, Jade E. Keehn, Andrew M. Durso, Susannah S. French, and Chris R. Feldman

PUBLISHED IN

Physiological and Biochemical Zoology 94, issue 1 (January/February 2021): 35–49

Jump/Scare

—

THALIA FIELD

Keywords: renewable energy, conservation physiology, reactive oxygen metabolites (dROMs), antioxidant capacity (OXY), trombiculid mite, anthropogenic disturbance

Scene one: exterior, Mojave Desert, day.

The side-blotched lizard may be common, but

"the global market for wind-generated power is growing faster than any other renewable energy source"[1]

and just because you're paranoid doesn't mean people aren't out to get you.

It's the lizard brain.

That small deep ancient part that functions to keep us on our toes.

Makes us hungry and afraid.

But the repetitive formula of science makes it less and less effective when it comes to surprise. We get lulled by the same old refrains, the same old methods, the same old tables and jargon and statistical regression.

---

1. N. Golait, R. M. Moharil, and P. S. Kulkarni, "Wind electric power in the world and perspectives of its development in India." *Renewable and Sustainable Energy Reviews* 13 (2009): 233–47; REN21. 2014. Renewables 2014 Global Status Report. REN21, Paris.

It's a myth, you know: the lizard brain was invented around the time when monster movies were most popular, and hit its peak when horror movies were hitting their stride.

The lizard brain seduced. After all, if people's behaviors could be blamed on something as alien as an internal ancestral reptile, we could certainly not be responsible for all our bloody mess.

Because fear is different than startle. Fear comes from uncertainty and not knowing the intention of the other. Fear is so primal. A startle is easy to induce.

We feel perplexed and unsure. We can't figure things out and nothing seems to resolve it. We get mixed signals.

Describing fear is as impossible as describing love, or power.

But common side-blotched lizards are real as you please, and their brains, honored by a few thieves in the desert below the thrum and woo of the turbines—are not that different than ours—just the same neural helmets donned proudly as we fumble through life's endless battlefield of bureaucracy.

The lizards seem miniscule from this angle, so far below, so far removed, so out of context to the jazz-hand robot clown-wheels in the sky. There's thud, woosh, and vibration. But nothing feels too out of place from the tiny lizard's point of view, nothing too disturbing. The distance between giant cartoonish turbine and tiny lizard, in a sunny shot-reverse-shot, seems almost funny.

Or so you think.

Panning down from the height where volant species suffer repeat violent encounters, from the height where the whale-white blades hammer through the sky-scraped wind-farmed air at up to 200 mph, from the height where hundreds of bald eagles and half a million other birds a year are killed in collisions with turbine blades—[2]

panning down, the drone connects the eagle's eye to the "fragile" desert floor and the mote of a lizard looking up at it.

Using inflatable car dealership dancing balloons would be a solution to save eagles from wind-farms, says an expert, because "eagles appear to be 'annoyed by anthropomorphic figures.'"

The dread of something happening is when the wind kicks up. Wind amplified through a small niche, the low-thwack soundtrack, the inescapable vibrations in the soil . . .

Something unusual despite everything *looking* just like any other desert day.

What was that?

Listening.

Wind.

Just wind.

But did something just move, a shadow? A quick slap of light against dark?

---

2. Eduardo Medina, "Wind energy company to pay $8 million in killings of 150 eagles," *The New York Times*, April 10, 2022. https://www.nytimes.com/2022/04/10/us/bald-eages -dead-wind-farms.html.

Again, there! Did you hear that?

The scientist types across the screen in saloon-style script, calming and reassuring:

Industrial Wind is here.

By 2050 it will be very much more here, to the tune of 35% of our energy, and very much here on the fragile desert floor and ceiling.

Wind "farms" make low-frequency noises from generators and blades.

Wind "farms" introduce humans and their roads and their trash and their disturbance and alteration of existing wildlife homes—

Wind "farms" increase species homogeneity thru loss of native habitat—

(and those bothersome dead eagles)

—but other than bothersome dead eagles, has anyone really *looked closely* at physiological stressors of the industrial wind?

Stress reduces ability to stay healthy, go dating and mating, live a good life, raise a family—

Oh, come on, you heard that! That wasn't just wind.

Stop.

Listen.

What if wind farms don't make life more stressful? What if the piles of metal junk create new homes? What if the restriction of traffic to the area decreases predation overall?

A shadow darts away.

Shhhhh!

Shouldn't we take a closer look?

Isn't that what scientists do? See something and take a closer look?

"Walking home along a desert road late at night" something is out of the ordinary. Something is amiss. Afoot. The whole scene becomes uncanny. Nothing is quite real.

We look where the shadow moved and the noise is loud.

Take a few steps.

Stop.

It all stops.

Silence.

Another step.

Stop.

A big turbine scoops in and out of frame.

Ok! It is just the wind turbines!

That's all it is.

What a relief.

It was just the turbines.

We can keep going. Resume normal walking.

The desert buzzes and hums.

Tracking shot builds a slow normal sense of calm, and the editing slows to one shot per minute.

Exhale.

The lizards get back to playing rock, paper, scissors . . . laughing among themselves:

It was only the feeling of "not being sure what's happening" of "going to look" because enough strange things made it not "quite normal" but also not clearly frightening—

but just when you test the right hypothesis—the open door, the radio left on—in that one off-guard moment, the terrifying thing jumps out of nowhere with a loud sound

SCREEECH!

A hand-held lizard-loop GRABS

tightens!

CAUGHT!

Common side-blotched lizards jump out of their skin by leaving their tail.

But it doesn't always work.

Scene two: interior, car trunk, day.

Lizards in burlap sacks bounce in the dark as the car careens between three wind farms and three control sites. Each lizard has been painfully labeled with a unique code. At each stop, a few more squirming sacks are tossed into the trunk.

Field Method: collect n=180 lizards over 6 days, "sampling" 2× per site per day. Captured a LOT more females than males.

Dust flies as the car spins off toward the isolated box of the Boyd Deep Canyon Desert Research Center. No one will know where you are. No one can hear you scream.

These lizards are good to study because they're sentimental about their little patch of earth, they don't run far or fast, and they are easy to catch in great numbers.

The scientist at the wheel whispers so the lizards can't hear.

We already know that the wind farms cause noise and human pollution . . . but . . . with the turbines, there are also fewer bird predators (high kill rates, anyone?) and so the lizards at the wind farms might be a little less bird-wary. Maybe they are having a better time of it—?

So are the wind farms good or bad? Could go either way!

A perfect scientific set up.

The best hypothesis is when you can make what's unseen or invisible do all the work for you. Keeps budgets down. No expensive monster makeup. Make it all out of pure fear. Implied bad guys. Pure dread. People are sick of girls tied up and having their tongues pulled out or eyes plucked. The question of each new era is—and our climate-ruining Anthropocene is no different—do we want real monsters, or monsters we can walk out of the theater and not believe exist?

"Let's check the oxidative balance—that's an established 'biomarker' for stress . . ."

Exactly! The blood concentration of reactive oxygen metabolites (dROMs) relative to the neutralizing capacity of blood antioxidants (Costantini 2014). Too many dROMs more than the natural oxidation capacity OXY means too much stress and might mean less reproduction and survival . . .

"Er, here we are," the researcher says, as they pull into the air-conditioned science habitat and begin piling sacks into carts.

Oxidative stress is also a compounding response to basically any issue: habitat disturbance, predation, resource depletion, air or noise pollution, urbanization—

"So," the other scientist interrupts, "let's check out oxidative stress by looking at ectoparasite load? Isn't that an associated disease-resistance issue—"

Who among us isn't an ectoparasite, you might joke, sipping your soda.

But, seriously, who are the ectoparasites?

Scene three: interior, field station, evening.

The scientists from above. Common side-blotched lizards outlined on a metal table.

Extreme-close-up on trombiculid mite grabbing one of the lizard's eyelids. Another has hold of a tail, a third latches on to a belly. Where they grab the skin looks irritated and shluffs off.

It's perfect misdirection. The nonfatal infection lasts about a week.

Assistants measure body size (snout-vent length, tail length, and mass).

Check.

They look for recent tail loss, because that could have something to do with something. Check.

Sex is noted, and if female, they palp the abdomen by hand, recording the number of yolked follicles, or what they casually refer to as "reproductive investment."

Check.

Then, finally, they count up the individual external parasites for each lizard using a handheld lens.

Extreme-close-up through handheld lens: A single waving trombiculid mite looks up!

Check!

Scene four: interior, storage container, day? night? who can tell.

Slow montage of lizards sitting around in metal cages, chilling, as it were, for, like, three days.

What about the acute stress of collection and short-term captivity?

Classic misdirection. That should have zero bearing on oxidative balance. Only really long stress exposure (i.e., multiple weeks of what you might call "glucocorticoid treatment") makes most vertebrates, including lizards, show something we can actually measure.

But for both acute and long-term stress, scientific method can "be an easy crutch to an unearned horror." Overused. On repeat. Try to control the variables. Invent cleverer and cleverer misdirections (not just another mirror trick; look behind you!) and put in scenes that feel entirely plausible, even routine, in the daily world of the audience. Add a dash of a fake solution to a pressing question.

"The noises stop, she thinks she's going to be ok."

"See, it's snowing! In a desert! Global warming isn't real."

Maybe you relax. Let your guard down. Eat a little popcorn.

Scene five: interior, car trunk, too dark to know what time it is.

After three days of "scientific efforts" the lizards are stuffed back into their sacks and driven to Utah State University where oxidative balance will finally be measured once and for all.

Scene six: interior, University of Utah laboratory, night.

Hurry up! Bags of lizards tossed to the arms of waiting assistants, the researchers frantically taking blood samples (via retro-orbital sinus capillary tube)—then rush the blood toward the ice cooler. There is literally no time to lose! Hurry you idiots! Get the blood plasma from the cells via centrifugation!

Now store the samples at 2207C.

Ok. Check. The scientists look around the room.

The lizards look around the room.

This is a completely different kind of desert. The wind turbines are nowhere to be seen.

Silence.

There is a sound but no idea where it's coming from.

Is that a creepy old-fashioned radio?

Some human breathing?

Something is moving.

The lizards' heads turn slowly.

Startles are common in mammals and reptiles, birds, and amphibians.

You might think a good science experiment is like a magic trick.

You know bad things are going to happen, but you don't know when.

Scientists who use the startle-type scare in a lab are "administering a startle probe."

A "bus" is when the scare turns out to be nothing—the feeling that after all, it's all ok, it was just a bus arriving! That that thing you thought wasn't real. That the fear you felt was just a dream or was all in your head. It's all ok. The music sounds sweet again, or at least quiet. You can go ahead and breathe. You can put the flowers on the grave. You can walk up the stairs. You can walk down the stairs. You can go outside. You can be in that boat. You can walk on the street in the evening. You can go to your garden. You can stand at your door. You can look out your window.

Scene seven: interior, University of Utah laboratory, early morning.

Red light illuminates the faces of scientists and lizards.

Basically the scientists didn't find any real difference in oxidative stress between any wind farm or control site location, except that pregnant females had higher oxidative stress no matter where they were captured, and there were statistically fewer mites on the lizards at the wind farms. But fewer mites is probably because the wind farms have the most cleared land, have gotten rid of most natural vegetation, which tends to breed insects. Anyway, it's all correlation. They can't show the cause.

Relax, this sort of *non-finding* is the normal state of "conservation physiology."

After all, oxidative stress is a simple stress response in general, so the scientists can't even account for all variables, they don't even *know* all the variables.

You know people who really love horror films. You know people who love doing scientific experiments. Both unfold in predictable ways, and yet for people who like them, it's the little details that make it work, the minor variations in how the data collection and suspense and statistics will occur. It's never really about the characters, though—if you think about it—they are simply the vessel for the feelings of the reader, they are the carriers of the atmosphere, the screen on which the real projection occurs. You can see a horror movie coming a mile away. From the first line, really. And the appearance of the lovely creature who you know won't make it to the end.

Scene eight: interior, University of Utah laboratory, a few minutes later.

Tight frame on lizard faces, one by one we pan across them in the red light. A high-pitched whine from the lightbulb can be heard, and the beating of a single heart.

The jump scare, that thing you have learned to expect after reading a hundred or more of these same reports, happens after a long sequence of suspense, or happens when it's quiet and no one expects anything. It is the laziest way to get your money's worth. It's too damn common. It's too damn boring. It's often used to place the antagonist suddenly in the scene, revealing the danger the protagonist is actually in, the proximity, the evaporation of the protective veil of ignorance.

Footsteps in the hall of the laboratory get louder.

Wide shot: the science building on the university campus in the light of day with crowds of students milling past, laughing and skipping.

A slammed door brings us back to:

Lizard point-of-view on one scientist's face.

What is she thinking? What are her hands doing?

A louder footstep. Stops.

Another scientist, smiling, pokes head around the corner of the slightly open door.

It's nothing. They're just chatting!

> "The startle process was described by two scientists, Landis and Hunt, in a classical study from 1932. . . . The purpose of the whole sequence, which typically takes about a second or less, is to protect vital organs and make the organism ready for confrontation with a threat. The eye-blink, which occurs as swiftly as 30–50 milliseconds after the startling stimulus, protects the eyes from trauma. It is followed by a widening of the eyes, which enlarges the visual field to allow for better threat assessment. The eyebrows shoot up to help open the eyes faster and wider. The mouth opens in a surprised O, probably to allow for a rapid intake of breath in anticipation of exertion. There is an almost-instantaneous up-regulation of the sympathetic nervous system, which is the branch of our autonomic nervous system that is responsible for the fight-or-flight response. Adrenaline and noradrenaline are released into the bloodstream, increasing heart rate and sweat secretion. The startle response is, in essence, an adaptive mechanism that prepares your system for action and tells you: Heads the fuck up!"[3]

No, no, relax, don't worry. That doesn't apply to this. These are just scientists who are looking into the effects of new technologies. They are our friends. They are protecting us from bad things that could happen, worse things than what we think is already bad that's happening. They

---

3. Mathias Clasen, *A Very Nervous Person's Guide to Horror Movies* (New York: Oxford University Press, 2021).

are asking important questions about the dangers of wind turbines. We need renewable energy but what harmful effects might these turbines be having?! Seriously, it's a good question.

Seriously, don't be afraid. Shut up and eat your popcorn.

Close-up on lizards sitting quietly.

The scientist types across the screen in saloon-style script, calming and reassuring:

"On completion of the study, we humanely euthanized all animals and preserved them as voucher specimens in the herpetology collection of the University of Nevada, Reno, Museum of Natural History (table S1)."

The growing use of artificial light at night, such as street lights, greenhouses, industrial facilities, and advertising columns, has the potential to increase the exposure of both aquatic and terrestrial organisms to continuous 24-hour photo-periods. This increase could be accompanied by light intensities and spectral compositions, but the real impact of the biological and ecological consequences of artificial night lighting is still unknown.

FROM
"Slowly Seeing the Light: An Integrative Review on Ecological Light Pollution as a Potential Threat for Mollusks"

BY
Ahmed A. A. Hussein, Erik Bloem, István Fodor, El-Sayed Baz, Menerva M. Tadros, et al.

PUBLISHED IN
Environmental Science and Pollution Research 28 (February 2021): 5036–48

Vortex

—

MIRANDA MELLIS

1.

night falls over the window
like an ink black curtain
we turn on the

light

is known
to be
inconstant, but upstart light's violent
aspect
is abstract
for those who live

inside

are
wrapped
in currents

don't know loss of night
nor grieve darkness nor miss
when night enveloped us in a coat of space
the darkening of this entire place

2.

small and drenched, washed whorls
eyes at the base of the tentacles
or
eyes on stalks

mollusk

pattern **detecting** light **receiving** shadow **mediating** direction
perceiving whole body **withdrawing** nocturnal **orientating**
light-zeitgeber **using**

the second
largest group
of animals
nonetheless

none the less

indistinct, in
conspicuous

sunless light	colonizing	shores of		space
spreading	cooptation	seeping		flickering
is invasive	invasive	invasive	violent	light

in light too

long

for darkness

Recent studies suggest that the disruption of animal chorus timing and organization is a consequence of increasing levels of anthropogenic noise in both terrestrial and aquatic ecosystems. However, it is not yet fully understood how anthropogenic activities influence animal chorusing at the population- and community-level across ecosystems worldwide. Urban ecosystems, especially, are characterized by multiple stressors, including chemical pollution, increasing temperature levels, high levels of anthropogenic noise (in both amplitude and frequency domains), artificial light at night (ALAN) and human presence, all of which can affect wildlife, with physiological, ecological and behavioral responses emerging to deal with such stressful conditions.

FROM
"A Global Synthesis of the Impacts of Urbanization on Bird Dawn Choruses"

BY
Oscar H. Marín-Gómez and Ian MacGregor-Fors

PUBLISHED IN
Ibis 163, issue 4 (October 2021): 1133–54

Words at Dawn Break

—

BETH PIATOTE

I.
According to scientists,
noise pollution forces
syntax change
in birdsong

so imagine
you've been hearing
   chick-a-dee-dee-dee

and then one
day, as dawn breaks,
you hear
   a-dee-chick-dee

and you awake
to a change
in the order of things

II.
The example above is flawed.
While it demonstrates a linguistic principle
of syntax change, it fails to account
for the fact that a chickadee signals
danger by adding more dees to its dee-dee-dee song

and surely the birds would have noted
a dee-dee-dee-dee-dee
situation

III.
Noise and light colonization
change the language
of some animals, including humans—
our elders bear this data
in their lungs

Sonic colonization
disrupts the animal chorus
ungrammars the tongue
breaks language into pieces
disorders the dawn

Amid the colonial noise
still we chorus animally
mourning light of silence
breaks
open into sound

Outside a crow is talking:
'áa'a híice 'áa'a híice 'áa'a!   *crow speaks crow speaks crow*
It sounds like breathing, the word
for crow—
when I say 'áa'a

I am speaking my language
and crow's. Through the noise
each dawn we hold safely
each other's language
in our mouths

As the Arctic warms at more than twice the global rate, advances in growing season phenology are likely to strongly influence the behavior of migratory caribou (*Rangifer tarandus*). Caribou are the dominant large herbivore in the Arctic and are ecologically important due to their effects on vegetation dynamics and socially important for providing subsistence food and cultural resources to rural and indigenous communities. . . . As the summer ranges of many Arctic caribou herds are being impacted by climate change and industrial development, there is a critical need to identify preferred habitat conditions, and understand how suitable habitat may be distributed in the future.

FROM

"Spring Phenology Drives Range Shifts in a Migratory Arctic Ungulate with Key Implications for the Future"

BY

John P. Severson, Heather E. Johnson, Stephen M. Arthur, William B. Leacock, and Michael J. Suitor

PUBLISHED IN

Global Change Biology 27, issue 19 (October 2021): 4546–63

Consider the Caribou

—

ELÉNA RIVERA

1.

Ask for a name

It migrates across barren-ground

It evolved to cope with short Arctic summers

"Snow shoveler," meaning pawed for food

Why the sudden quote marks around "wild animal"?

Known by many related wayward designations

Which is the one known by its "velvet" antlers?

2.

Based around montane surroundings
    It makes large-scale shifts in space patterns
        The mapping of the page, the language of air

Migration can shift all universes
    —the influence of climate (no way to climb out of it)
        on the yearly phenomena of timing and seasons

3.

Spring desire drives large-scale
range shifts in terms of space-use
Key to variations in nourishment
because of the need to acclimate
to early vegetation growth

Relationships now guide the way
In the future the herd will follow
the fabric of the current climate—
an itinerant traces displacement
and depends on population size

4.

Trekked further north, where there are songs

and tended "to avoid industrial development"

Recent plans to produce oil could alter

Extreme shifts in space use predicted

5.

Disturbance in a landscape
extends to the interior life

A difficult voyage
Look back at what'll be culled

Some species already extinct
During the short window available

6.

Snow melt
Riverine, rills, runnels
The receding heart edge
Moving from region to region
"Adapt or die" then there's insect harassment
Hardness in landscapes still brown or snow covered

7.

What will the habitat allow
pre-calving and post-calving?
Sea ice recedes and mottled
pastures change in such a time
Already the tendency to wander
There's also human disturbance

8.

Respond to patterns, the charged air

Moving changes the available balance

becomes a pattern inside an assertion

The tall shrub, the low shrubs, a slope

access to immature cotton grass flowers

strange shadows   sense the now melt

9.

During seasonal change
make spacial adjustments
for the ghosts of this poem
Warmer weather emergence
enters and harasses the map

Common Eastern Bumble Bee *(Bombus impatiens)*

FOOD

—

All organisms require energy to survive. Many animals get it by eating algae, lichens, plants, or each other. Other animals, such as corals, generate energy symbiotically. The animals you see most often—ants, cockroaches, rats, squirrels, sparrows, and people—are those that eat almost anything and can adapt readily to new food sources.

Humans are by far the most successful animal when it comes to acquiring energy. For one thing, we are omnivores. Our ability to cook food gives us another big advantage: cooking renders more types of foods edible, increases our ability to extract calories from each meal, and lets us store more food than, for example, a squirrel hiding a nut. Additionally, we can hunt, grow, package, and transport our food in large quantities.

Many species are also capable of changing their diets depending on what is available. Polar bears will eat goose eggs if they cannot hunt seals once the sea ice melts. Bears, coyotes, crows, foxes, and raccoons learn to raid our garbage cans; birds and insects learn to infest our crops. Wolves and other predators kill cattle, sheep, and goats, even though extreme weather is a more common cause of livestock death. Rabbits and deer feed on our gardens.

Interestingly, closely related species often eat different things. Northern orcas regularly catch multiple species of salmon; southern orcas go only for the Chinook. Long-tailed weasels prey on everything from bird eggs to snakes to snowshoe hares, while their relatives, the black-footed ferrets, eat only prairie dogs.

—*Lucy Spelman*

The Northern Resident-type killer whale (NRKW) population, numbering about 120 whales in the 1970s, increased nearly continuously at about 2 percent, now numbering about 300 whales. Conversely, although the southernmost group of fish-eating killer whales, the Southern Resident killer whales (SRKW) did gradually increase though the mid-1990s, a 20 percent decline that occurred through 2001 and prompted the listing of the population under the U.S. Endangered Species Act (ESA) and Canadian Species at Risk Act (SARA), and the population has fluctuated since then. SRKWs provide an example of an endangered predator whose diet largely comprises a threatened prey species. The SRKW population currently consists of 74 individual whales and is comprised of three largely matrilineal groups, referred to as pods with alphabetic identifications (i.e., J, K, and L). Most populations of Chinook salmon along the west coast of the United States are themselves listed as threatened or endangered under the ESA, and are harvested in commercial, recreational, and tribal fisheries. Simultaneously achieving recovery of this predator and its prey while sustaining viable fisheries presents a significant management challenge.

FROM

"Endangered Predators and Endangered Prey:
Seasonal Diet of Southern Resident Killer Whales"

BY

M. Bradley Hanson, Candice K. Emmons, Michael J. Ford,
Meredith Everett, Kim Parsons, et al.

PUBLISHED IN

PLoS ONE 16, issue 3 (2021): 1–27

Orca Oracle

—

KAZIM ALI

There are three different kinds of killer whales in the Pacific, genetically distinct. The resident whales live in large family structures close to the coast, the transient whales wander out into the ocean in much smaller groups, and far out, relatively recently discovered are larger populations of offshore whales.

There are 274 resident killer whales in the Pacific northwest, 200 in the northern group and 74 in the southern group. The southern group is roughly gathered into three matrilineal pods.

In this case, both predator and prey are endangered. And what happens when the prey is also of commercial value. Who wins.

The plot of *Star Trek IV: The Voyage Home* revolved around an apocalypse being caused by the extinction of the humpback whale. An alien probe has arrived to investigate why it no longer hears the communications of the whale song which somehow amplified into space. The ridiculously named George and Gracie are set free only to be hunted by whalers. The climactic battle of the film is not with Klingons or Khan but with a whaling ship.

Only the summer diets of the killer whales have been studied. The northern resident whales mostly occupy the shores of British Columbia, while the southern resident whales range from Washington down the California coast.

I moved to California from Ohio in 2019, not sure I would ever move back across the Continental Divide again. Humans are animals too, but we do not often stop to think about where we want to range or what food we need to eat for our own survival. For the one, we just follow the money. For the other we follow our appetite, which is never deep within our body but just on the surface of the tongue.

The Salish Sea and the Puget Sound yielded up results to the scientists: prey remains and fecal samples, to be able to understand how the killer whales were surviving, what it might be (coho salmon or Chinook salmon) we were taking out of their mouths.

It turns out chum salmon were the second-most common prey. I call my partner "Cham" (pronounced "chum"), which is short for "chamcha," the urdu word for *spoon*. It's normally an insult in urdu, used to refer to someone who's a sidekick or a hanger-on, but we started calling each other by this name after reading *The Satanic Verses,* in which one of the characters' names is Chamchawalla, which he tries to shorten and anglicize as Chamcha. It's not meant to be complimentary in the novel, either.

It's the Chinook salmon that is the most common prey species for the whales, the Chinook who swim from the sea up the river to mate. I moved up the river too, from New York City to Rhinebeck, which is where I met my chamcha. Chinooks, who are named for the Chinookan Indigenous people of the Pacific Northwest.

The Chinook Nation is still seeking federal recognition, which had been granted under President Bill Clinton in the last days of his presidency but revoked by the Bush administration.

Even though *The Satanic Verses* came out in 1988, I did not read it until 2002, afraid of the book somehow, afraid of what I would feel about it. What I feel about it is that it is brilliant, strange, and provocative. I heard

Rushdie on a radio call-in show describing it as an argument for secular humanism. I called in to the show to tell him that while I thought it was a remarkable exploration of faith and how and why we believe the things we believe, I did not agree with him that in the end calculus it argued for secular humanism.

I do not now remember his reply.

Chum salmon are so-called from the Chinook word *tzum* meaning "marked."

I am marked as different in my own family, first tried to evade, then tried to rise above, now I travel among them, marked but cheerful.

While Scotty tries to fabricate a plastic that would enable the construction of a tank for the many hundreds of tons of water required to transport George and Gracie through time back to Starfleet Headquarters, Uhura and Chekov are trying to steal a nuclear reactor from a submarine to power the warp engines of the stolen Klingon ship.

The science from science-fiction shows is always a metaphor for social anxieties or political crises at the time: warp speed, transporter technology, artificial intelligence, virtual reality.

The scientists who were tracking the prey of the killer whales could tell you where the prey came from, what stocks of fish it descended from, what its makeup was.

The Chinook is a warm western wind. When I moved to California, I moved to a city on a mesa, between the ocean and the mountains, in the traditional land of the Kumeyaay people, whose territories spanned what is now the U.S.–Mexico border.

Humans and animals don't know borders really. We drew them on the map. It is tempting to say they aren't "real," but if you go down to the border near the city where I live, you can see how water distribution and terrain reconstruction have created two vastly different ecosystems on either side of the slatted, barricaded fence.

Music drifts over from Tijuana, whose neighborhoods extend flush against the fence. Which extends outwards, hundreds of yards, into the sea.

Saladin Chamcha is enraged all the time but suppresses his rage. He slowly, during the course of the novel, begins transforming into a horned and hooved monster, a devil.

When the Chinook is more available—in the summer months—it is the preferred diet of the whales. In the other seasons, chum salmon, halibut, lingcod, and other fish become larger parts of the whales' diet.

Paul Crutzen coined the term "Anthropocene" at the beginning of the millennium to define an age in the planet where ecosystems were impacted primarily by human endeavor. In 2016, Donna Haraway started using the (intentionally misspelled) term "Chthulucene" to imply that whatever humans had wrought has now traveled quite beyond them. That things were out of our control. That human and nonhuman were not bound together inextricably.

One could not only learn about the whales' diets from studying their fecal matter but one also learned how far from their natal rivers the salmon traveled.

Because the *Enterprise* crew has traveled so far into the past to find the whales, they make humorous mistakes in their misunderstandings of technology. Chekov's Russian accent gets him in trouble as a suspected spy. Scotty tries to fabricate the plastic by speaking to the computer. "Computer?" he asks brightly. The technician hands him a mouse and says, "You have to use this." Scotty holds the mouse up and in that same bright voice once again asks, "Computer?"

There is, of course, no answer.

Throughout my life I moved from place to place. The longest I've lived anywhere are the ten years I spent in Ohio from my mid-thirties to my mid-forties, and the whole time I was there I was traveling, living for months at a time in other places.

Home is a wandering for me, or at least it always had been, until I crossed the Continental Divide and arrived on the western shore.

So what if George and Gracie were borne through time to save the future—in the present, our present, they still went extinct. We lost them.

247 resident killer whales does not seem like that many killer whales.

It's not a food chain, it's a food web. The building of a dam in northern Canada impacted the water, the fish, beaver, moose, muskrat, trees, and so on. Water flows.

The "satanic" verses of the titles are the ones that Lucifer supposedly slipped into the Quran when no one was looking. So you wouldn't know whose words were god's and whose were not.

In the Chthulucene there's no scripture or road map for what happens next. How can we manage salmon populations to support the southern resident killer whales. What impact will that have on other predator species.

And we now have to figure out how to manage prey species populations for endangered apex predators.

In a family, some stay close to shore, some wander out and return, and others head for open sea.

Perhaps the answers are written somewhere in the sacred laws of the past or in the dizzying regulations and legislation of the present or the sympoiesis between human and nonhuman. As the scientists finally conclude, "Further research is needed."

Computer? Computer?

Polar bears depend on a robust under-ice ecosystem that supports their primary prey, ringed *(Pusa hispida)* and bearded seals *(Erignathus barbatus)*, as well as regionally variable secondary prey, such as beluga whales *(Delphinapterus leucas)* and walruses *(Odobenus rosmarus)*. Changes that occur within the ecosystem, including regional contaminant levels and reductions in sea ice algae, can be detected in polar bears. Furthermore, in places where polar bears have exhibited population declines, other species within the system have also exhibited declines in body condition and vital rates.

FROM

"Seal Body Condition and Atmospheric Circulation Patterns
Influence Polar Bear Body Condition, Recruitment,
and Feeding Ecology in the Chukchi Sea"

BY

Karyn D. Rode, Eric V. Regehr, Jeffrey F. Bromaghin,
Ryan R. Wilson, Michelle St. Martin, et al.

PUBLISHED IN

Global Change Biology 27, issue 12 (June 2021): 2684–701

Wonderful

—

ANNIE HARTNETT

Bill has always been sensitive, which explains why he stays off the internet. He doesn't like to know sad things. His wife, his lovely wife Edith, respects this. Every morning Edith gets up before Bill, and she pads downstairs in her slippers and she gets the newspaper off the walk, and then she takes the scissors to it. Bill wants to read the paper, wants to be informed, but he doesn't want to know sad things. He is too sensitive. His heart can't take it, he and his wife agree. He is almost seventy, and he has had three heart attacks. A fourth might be the one to do it. So, every morning, she cuts up the paper. She takes out the sad things, the horrible, the terrible. By the time Bill gets the paper, it is in tatters. They started this years ago, before the heart attacks, actually, and before the internet, back when their daughter was born. It was 1986. They thought things were bad then. Chernobyl. The *Challenger* space shuttle. And of course things only got worse, after the 90s.

At first, Edith didn't think it was a bad thing, to protect her sensitive husband. He could still do his job as a handyman. He was useful around the house. He was a loving father to Rachel, back when she lived at home.

"Wonderful day, isn't it," he says to Edith, every morning. Every single morning he says it, right after he's done with his coffee.

Edith is the only one to read the emails that arrive from their daughter, and she tells Bill what she can. She tells him the good bits, how their daughter met someone, there is a cute guy on the recent research trip, and he's planning to divorce his wife, they just need to work out the details with the kids. He's pretty much single, Rachel promises her mother, in the emails. When Edith relays this to Bill, about Rachel's new man, she leaves out the divorce part. Leaves out the children. The guy is free as a bird for all Bill knows. Bill says he's glad she's found someone, it must be lonely up there. Their daughter is in Alaska. Bill wishes she would live at home, with him and Edith, but Rachel is thirty-five years old and she lives in Alaska but she regularly goes on expeditions even further into the Arctic. If you can believe it, their daughter rides in a helicopter and shoots polar bears with a dart gun full of tranquilizers and then she measures them and figures out if they've had enough to eat and if the bears are thriving or if they are suffering.

But all Bill knows, all Bill really understands, is that Rachel is a wild-life biologist, and she studies polar bears for a living. Bill is very proud of her. Any father would be. Even if it would be nice if she didn't live so far from home. Alaska is a long trip.

There is nothing in this entire world sadder than polar bears, Edith wants to tell her husband, because of course Bill doesn't get it. The polar bears will either drown because the sea ice is gone, or they will starve because the seals will go first, their main food source. Whatever way the bears will die out, Edith is sure that way will be terrible. Extinction is coming, eventually, for polar bears. The newspaper has made that clear, and Edith cuts those articles out and tosses them out before Bill sees them. She even threw away one where Rachel herself was quoted. She couldn't risk it, her husband seeing it, what Rachel said about those poor bears, and how they were doing okay for now, at least the bears in this one region were, but they couldn't survive "limitless loss of their sea ice habitat." As far as Bill knows, the polar bears have plenty of ice, Rachel's new boyfriend isn't married to someone else, this new boyfriend also doesn't have two kids with another woman who is not Rachel, and Bill thinks his wife Edith is happy and has always been happy. The newspaper comes in the morning, the coffee is hot, the orange juice has no pulp. Everything is wonderful.

Black-footed ferrets rely predominantly on prairie dogs (*Cynomys spp.*) for food, as well as utilizing their burrows for shelter. As specialist predators, 60–90% of the ferret's diet comprises prairie dogs. However, between the late 1800s and 1960, prairie dog numbers dramatically declined due to habitat destruction, expansion of non-native sylvatic plague, and poisoning. Consequentially, ferret numbers declined precipitously and have been the subject of intensive conservation efforts, including captive breeding and reintroduction, ever since.

FROM

"Environmental and Prey-based Factors Underpinning Variability in Prairie Dogs Eaten by Black-footed Ferrets"

BY

Ellen S. Dierenfeld, Katherine Whitehouse-Tedd, Veronique Dermauw, Louis R. Hanebury, and Dean E. Biggins

PUBLISHED IN

Ecosphere 12, issue 1 (January 2021): 1–19

Prairie Dog Proceedings

—

ROBIN MCLEAN AND TIM SUTTON

Court of the High Prairie Dog Town
PD District 111113

Case Number PD4598PDH

Prosecution, The High Prairie Dog Counsel
Represented by, The Right Honorable PD Quick, Esquire

v.

Defendants, ELLEN S. DIERENFELD, KATHERINE WHITEHOUSE-TEDD,
VERONIQUE DERMAUW, LOUIS R. HANEBURY, AND DEAN E. BIGGINS

Represented by: The Right Honorable BF Ferret, Esquire.

In the matter of the crime of

HIGH and AGGRAVATED MURDER, multiple counts

Findings after Evidentiary Hearing & Recommendations
for Further Action

History

Hear ye, Hear ye, now comes the Court of the High Prairie Dog with
findings following the preliminary hearing of Defendants: ELLEN S.
DIERENFELD, KATHERINE WHITEHOUSE-TEDD, VERONIQUE DERMAUW,

LOUIS R. HANEBURY, AND DEAN E. BIGGINS, hereafter called *Dierenfeld et al.*, or Defendants. The aforesaid Defendants were apprehended (after long search given obvious obstructions to pursuit and assistance by affiliates) and are currently in custody in a highly secured subsurface facility in the northern PD District 111113 (their so-called "Wyoming") where they were deemed in prior hearing to be ineligible for bail and pretrial release due both to flight risk and for their own safety pending trial, given the current unstable "mood" stirring in so many of our Communities ignited by such (alleged) acts of (alleged) brutal violence toward Prairie Dogs, acts that have been deemed inconsequential by (hominid, omnivorous) megafauna for eons in and around our Towns. Defendants currently await trial for the multiple counts of High Murder (premeditated murder with intent and extreme prejudice), PDS 25.45(d) in the West Continental Jurisdiction.

Counsel for *Dierenfeld et al.* moved on March .75, Çꙥ&ꙥ for Summary Judgment in her clients' favor, seeking relief from this Court from the serious charges against them. A hearing was granted and lengthy (we might add, very contentious, not to say *gruesome*) evidence (Exhibits 1a through 15c) was submitted to this Court on August 346.2 of the same Solar Year related to the underlying facts. Defense Counsel initially asserted that all charges should be dropped against her clients based on one or all of the following defense(s): (1) Prejudice, (2) Justification (3) Vagueness, (4) Unspecificity, (5) Necessity.

This Court, of course, has heard such defenses before in similar instances. Fortunately, precedent is crystal clear as to our duty to dispatch such specious efforts at subverting justice.

Facts

The facts of this case are (amazingly) not in dispute. Between July 1988 and March 1989 (hominid time) *Dierenfeld et al.* admit to killing an unspecified number of Prairie Dogs in various districts of their so-called

Western North America in order to study the Prairie Dogs' corpses' physical composition for the purpose of calculating the nutritional value of ingestion Prairie Dogs by black-footed ferrets. *Dierenfeld et al.* are quite specific and unabashed about their acts in sworn testimony. They freely admit to having employed "trained marksmen ensur[ing] that prairie dogs were shot in a manner that minimized suffering and did not impact sympatric species." (How *Dierenfeld et al.* can claim to murder innocents [and total strangers] in cold blood while also asserting they are "minimizing suffering" is frankly mystifying, but not a matter for this Court at this time; it is rather a concern for ethicists and philosophers, we believe, with artists likely leading the way, since—while it is well known that even the smallest death generates tiny but potent ripples in overlapping waves of distortion in all directions *out out out* from suffering *in situ*—it yet falls to the conceptual, artistic, and theoretical thinkers [rather than we, the operators of the blunt mechanisms of the law] to conceive of ways and means of conveying such weighty yet ephemeral concepts effectly to the ignorant.) However, what happened to the Prairie Dog victims *after* their admitted murders at issue here is equally shocking to the conscience of this Court.

In direct testimony *Dierenfeld et al.* waxed eloquent about the methods employed for ascertaining the nutritional value of Prairie Dogs to the (apparently more precious) black-footed ferrets. *Dierenfeld et al.* referred to "sample preparations" and coolly listed their acts performed on the unfortunate corpses of their victims. We quote here from the hearing record to demonstrate the peculiar, if somewhat robotic, language used by the Defendants and that we believe is illuminating as to state of mind:

> Each individual was assigned an ID number, and species, sex, age class, season, and collection site were recorded for each animal in the field. Dead prairie dogs were transported on ice and processed at NERC. Efforts were made to prepare the prairie dog carcasses in a manner reflecting the portion consumed by ferrets.

Although detailed investigations of ferret feeding behavior were lacking at the time of sampling, field observations indicated that the feet and anterior skull (nose and teeth; herein referred to as "face") were often rejected. As such, these were cut off, weighed (all weights to the nearest 0.1 g), and then discarded. Carcasses were skinned, and the skin weighed. Since skin was particularly difficult to prepare for chemical analysis (i.e., grinding), only one skin from each age class per location was saved and frozen for further processing/analysis; all other skins were discarded. The remainder of the carcass (i.e., reflecting the consumed components), including brain and digestive tract tissues plus contents, was weighed and recorded. Next, the entire gastrointestinal tract (esophagus through anus) was removed intact. To examine potential variability in prairie dog diets across sites, stomach contents (when present) were removed in toto and weighed separately. Five g of stomach contents were placed into labeled plastic bags with 5 mL of 25 percent sodium-ascorbate solution for vitamin analysis; any residual stomach contents were stored in a separate, labeled bag for later proximate and mineral composition analysis. The intestinal tract was then stripped of contents into a separate container, before the entire gastrointestinal tissue was weighed, and tissue placed back into the carcass sample. . . . The entire carcass (including gastrointestinal tract tissues, less contents) was ground through a meat grinder four times into a homogenous mixture; 5 g of carcass mixture was placed into labeled plastic bags with 5 mL of 25 percent sodium ascorbate solution for vitamin analysis, and a separate 20-g carcass sample was stored in a separate bag for later proximate and mineral composition analyses. Previously frozen skins were ground through a meat grinder, and 20 g subsamples taken and placed into labeled plastic bags. All labels, associated subsamples, and data sheets were double-checked for completeness and consistency and stored frozen at $-20°C$ for no longer than 6 months before overnight shipment to the Nutrition Laboratory, Wildlife Health Center at the New York Zoological Society (Bronx, New York, USA).

Needless to say, it was a grisly business.

Predictably, this testimony was unsettling to this Court (and explosive to and for the Towns and Towns of Prairie Dog Protestors gathered at mounds and subsurface spheres outside, around, and under the detention facility, witnessing and outraged by the bits and pieces of these hearings that inevitably leaked out [despite best efforts] via roots, branches, insects, and chemical tendrils). Defendants predictably elected to exercise their right Against Self-Incrimination in the tumult, but did so well after their admissions of murder, mutilation, and grinding of Prairie Dogs were "out of the bag." Concurrently, Defense Counsel sought to mitigate the damning power of her clients' testimony by claiming that *Dierenfeld et al.* (1) didn't actually kill the victims themselves, but hired "a marksman" to do so, and (2) that Defendants were hired *only* to "gather nutritional research" and therefore lacked requisite intent to kill for conviction for the most serious charges. Whatever (small) persuasive power these legal maneuvers might have enjoyed was swiftly quashed by corroborating documentary evidence submitted by the Prosecution, wherein Defendants can indeed be said to have "crowed in print" about the murders and mutilation (grinding up) of an unspecified number of Prairie Dogs in a noted hominid periodical called *Ecosphere* (attached herein). In what is now famous, and some might deem "infamous," materials, the Court accepted into evidence the article entitled: *"Environmental and prey-based factors underpinning variability in prairie dogs eaten by black-footed ferrets"* (Exhibit 1d). It is an innocent enough sounding title. We grant this. It sounds like a research project for the benefit of the black-footed ferret, an endangered species that current hominids have wiped out by standard and repetitious habitat reduction. It is a sad old song this Court is all too familiar with. (Note: Defense Counsel vigorously objected to admission of the article into evidence given article's immediately obvious persuasive power and—she argued—"clearly prejudicial nature." But we have ruled time and time again in favor of admission of prejudicial evidence as long as it is also clearly "relevant and necessary." Such is the case here, while too, we know, "Death is death." *See also* Rufus v. High Prairie Dog Counsel, *PD District 3.t7.*)

The hearing concluded, and despite the burdensome task of having to reconsider the horror of the underlying evidence, this Court knows what "duty" is and what is asked of moral beings. As required, we did reencounter and reconsider the dizzyingly dramatic (and murderous) evidence against *Dierenfeld et al.* in the intervening weeks and months since the hearing, have employed every effort to be "fair" and "open minded" to the Defendants, but even more so to follow the Law of the Prairie Dog, the Law of The Town, even as the Prairie Dog Community at large has screamed for blood "at the gates" of the subsurface facility where the Defendants are still housed. We know our job.

Our findings are to be found here as follows:

Findings

Whereas: Dierenfeld et al. admit in Exhibit 1a (albeit using the passive voice, as is common with hominids):

> between the late 1800s and 1960, prairie dog numbers dramatically declined due to habitat destruction, expansion of non-native sylvatic plague [aka red death; aka ferret fever; aka "The Badlands"], and poisoning (Fish and Wildlife Service 2013a). Consequentially, ferret numbers declined precipitously and have been the subject of intensive conservation efforts, including captive breeding and reintroduction, ever since. (p. 2, para 3)

Whereas: Aforementioned "habitat destruction" took the form of ongoing, persistent, perseverant, and wanton extirpation of vibrant Prairie Dog Towns and the Communities therein.

Whereas: This Court has previously recognized the extended genocide experienced by our sworn enemies, the black-footed ferret. (See Blackback v. High Prairie Dog Counsel, *PD District 45.h3.*) And that the chief cause of said genocide has been the aforementioned assault on Our Towns by hominids.

Whereas: This Court has previously ruled against the "chocolate laxative" defense, wherein the cause of a disease is prescribed as its cure. (See Purplespeckledback v. High Prairie Dog Counsel, *PD District 12.v2.* ÇŽÞØ.) The relevance to the current case is that the decline of our enemies, the black-footed ferrets, is entirely the result of the destruction of Prairie Dog Towns. Shooting, and then grinding up *yet more* Prairie Dogs (no matter how nutritious) cannot have the desired effect.

Therefore: The Court of the High Prairie Dog Town, PD District 111113 advises expansion of the current borders of all Towns located within the Districts, and long-distance communication of these findings and recommendations to all Towns in Neighboring Districts. It is the opinion of this Court that only by reinhabiting territories lost to hominid predation will the "ecosphere," as the hominids refer to it (we all know the topside is neither flat nor round, but bumpy. And hominids barely even recognize the below ground as part of their "sphere"), be able to support the expansion of either Prairie Dogs or black-footed ferret communities. That this may reignite past conflicts between ferrets and Prairie Dogs, the Court is aware, but our advice is to dig that tunnel when the time comes.

Conclusion

For all these reasons noted, Defense Counsel's Motions for Summary Judgment is DENIED.

Swift foxes *(Vulpes velox)* are currently distributed in isolated short- and mixed-grass prairies, and surrounding ancillary landscapes, throughout the Great Plains, which remain patchy and vulnerable to conversion. They were once extirpated across large portions of their distribution in North America (e.g., bounties, poisoning), but have re-established populations across their native range where they remain at low densities (0.16–0.31 swift fox/km^2). Grassland availability may be the most important factor to swift fox survival and likely influential at dispersal-scale distances ($\bar{x} = 15$ km). Swift fox primarily prey upon small mammals, insects, and birds and construct burrows in suitable loamy soils to avoid predation and raise kits. The eastern edge of swift fox contemporary distributions, where landscape change is likely most prolific, has become a patchy matrix of grazed and un-grazed remnant native grasslands, intensive row-crop agriculture, and energy development.

FROM

"Strategic Grassland Conservation for Swift Foxes
in Multi-use Landscapes"

BY

Ty J. Werdel, Colleen W. Piper, Andrew M. Ricketts,
Matthew S. Peek, Dan S. Sullins, and Adam A. Ahlers

PUBLISHED IN

Biological Conservation 277 (January 2023): 1–9

Swift Foxes in Kansas Grasses, Five Fields

—

ELENI SIKELIANOS

If it is not ice, it is rock.
If it is not rock, it is dirt.
If it is dirt and not ocean, it should have grasses.
If it is not wolf it is fox.
If it is not swift it is glow.
If it is grass it is growing.
And foxes go swishing through   *swift swift*   tawny tips
        of tails mix with tawny grasses' switches
a *Vulpes velox,* velourish in the tumblegrass
catching its own biofuel in the side-oats grama
        needs so little in bird or grasshopper
and a grassland that has never been ripped   at its root
    /from its socle/   is different
in nutrient and news   from one that has had its works unbedded
    /grassonomy smashed

∴

None of us knows our fate, yet scientists say swift foxes
have known-fate survivance
so tied to grasses
so — easy: let the grasses grow

∴

to share your dinner with a swift fox, put away the corn, defold the field,
     don't plant the seed, leave the grass unpulled, dirt untilled
cultivate your taste for mice and crickets, stinkbugs, berries

∴

Everyone has a fox story.

S. told me how the kit foxes played jokes on her, stole clothes from her
tent and hid them behind rocks, laughed as they watched her hunt for
her woolens in the morning.

L. told me of a fox who curled up under her window in Berlin and spent
the night. That's just a German fox, you might say, an urban *Vulpes*
living off trash. In the morning, the fox yawned, stretched an ocher
stretch, took its time, and trotted off.

∴

witchgrass always puts me in a panicum, worrying

is there a chirp in extirpation?
no, a long low moan   too deep to hear
it's the earth   from which the grasses grow   buffalo grass
     bluestem   dropseed
where the mices swift foxes hunt hide   and when one voluptuous
     Vulpes light
goes out the wide   panicked grama sea   witches itself

A single worker of *B. borealis* was observed in July in the northeast of the state, apparently the first sighting in Ohio since the 1950s, according to records from the Cleveland Museum of Natural History Insect Collection and the C. A. Triplehorn Insect Collection at the Ohio State University (specimen verified and vouchered at the Cleveland Museum of Natural History). We did not observe two species of particular conservation concern that were historically found in Ohio *(B. afnis* and *B. terricola),* despite intensive survey effort and inclusion of suitable habitat in and near locations where they were most recently sighted.

FROM

"Bumble Bee Species Distributions and Habitat Associations in the Midwestern USA, a Region of Declining Diversity"

BY

Jessie Lanterman Novotny, Paige Reeher, Megan Varvaro, Andrew Lybbert, Jesse Smith, et al.

PUBLISHED IN

Biodiversity and Conservation 30 (February 2021): 865–87

A Single Worker

—

MAGGIE SMITH

Where, blond bee, are the rest
    of your kind—where,

        yellow-haired hum,
    where, fur & bristle & buzz?

Alone in the clover, you appear
    to be a tiny queen,

        a shrunken version
    of the one you tend to,

like a child feeding her mother. Where
    is she? What door in a tree

        stands ajar for you?
    What hollow holds

the royal you'll bumble
    back to, pollen caught

        in your fuzz the color
    of sun? Northern amber,

bright whir, may a swarm wait,
    thrumming, for your return.

Polybrominated diphenyl ethers (PBDEs) were introduced in the 1970s as flame retardants, and their extensive use, persistence in the environment, and bioaccumulative properties have resulted in widespread contamination of water, wildlife, and humans. The toxic effects of PBDEs include disruption of thyroid and immune functions and possible deleterious effects on behavioral development and reproduction. . . . Concentrations of PBDEs in wildlife in some areas of North America leveled off or began decreasing in the early 2000s. Nonetheless, PBDEs are present in many products still in use, including textiles, plastics, insulation, and electronics, and their disposal and degradation continue to release PBDEs into the environment. Atmospheric transport and deposition allow PBDEs to reach remote locations, and due to past contamination, lake and stream sediments and water from tributaries also act as sources of PBDEs.

FROM

"Patterns and Trends of Polybrominated Diphenyl Ethers
in Bald Eagle Nestlings in Minnesota and Wisconsin, USA"

BY

William T. Route, Cheryl R. Dykstra, Sean M. Strom,
Michael W. Meyer, and Kelly A. Williams

PUBLISHED IN

Environmental Toxicology and Chemistry 40,
issue 6 (June 2021): 1606–18

Fire Sermon

—

MARCO WILKINSON

I don't want to die. Burning in my bed. Burning in my car. Burning in my brain, my mind enthralled with a world one hairsbreadth apart from the one I live in. And so, fearing burning, I burn with a desire not to burn. So I sleep in organobromides called polybrominated diphenyl ethers. So I drive down the road in organobromides called polybrominated diphenyl ethers. So I take this externalized mind called the internet exploding with the firing synapses of billions of people here and now and accumulating in electricity the blazing heat of human civilization and I encase it in a thin rectangle of organobromides called polybromide diphenyl ethers.

I am in a world. I am made of a world. I understand comfort in it and make my way through it and piece together a picture of it and feel myself safe in it (so safe I didn't even know I was in danger) and store momentary mock-ups of it and feel my body in relation to it. It is a cold fire that keeps me.

Since the 1970s, polybrominated diphenyl ethers (PBDEs) have been used as flame retardants in a wide variety of household goods, from furniture padding and upholstery, to plastics used in automobiles and electronic devices. I was born in 1976 into a PBDE world. I spent the 1980s staring at televisions whose plastic casings exhaled PBDEs on couches whose foam padding exhaled PBDEs or played board games with my cousins splayed out on plush living room carpets that exhaled PBDEs on nights when the curtains drawn against the cold exhaled PBDEs. Do PBDEs have an odor? I don't know, but when I think back to my childhood it is nothing but a disconcertingly vivid symphony of outgasses. PBDEs kept me safe from the carpet catching fire (I remember jumping from couch to chair to love seat with my cousin as a little kid—"The floor is lava!"). PBDEs kept me safe from the TV exploding (I remember the video of a man being beaten by police, beaten and beaten and beaten). PBDEs kept me safe from couches flaming up around me (I remember in high school sitting next to my best friend on his couch and wanting nothing more than to kiss him, and so I did; he was so kind in his rejection).

Smell or no smell, signal of their presence or no signal, PBDEs have been shedding from the skin of my world like ash slipping away from the surface of an ember on the updrafts of combustion all this time. Weak chemical bonds mean they slip into the stream: the stream of water tumbling through a washing machine's rinse cycle or percolating through a landfill; the stream of bacteria drinking that water in through a skin that is all mouth and always thirsty; the stream of protozoa hungrily turning bacteria into themselves; the stream of fish streaming water and bacteria and protozoa and plankton and microplastics through their mouths and gills; the stream of raptor talons that rake through the stream and in a flash of scale and water and light lift fish whole out of their world into the air and an aerie. PBDEs stream out of our world and into theirs: bacteria and protozoa and fish and eagles.

The people most likely to be affected by PBDEs are those who work in the factories and plants where they are impregnated into the various plastic casings and foam pads and upholstery fabrics that forgettably crowd our lives, or those who work in recycling facilities where all these items are shuttled to for some potential future reuse. They are most likely to inhale contaminated dust generated by the manufacturing or disassembly process, like the ash blown off a raging fire burning to keep us from burning. The effects are varied, ranging from neurotoxicity to endocrine toxicity. (Bromides were once used as sedatives in the late nineteenth and early twentieth centuries, though later abandoned due to the development of bromism, a syndrome of memory loss and tremors, schizophrenia and a certain cognitive dullness. Bromides: those insipid catch-all phrases meant to placate and soothe.)

PBDEs vary based on the amount of bromine in a given molecule. Higher brominated molecules bind more easily with soils and sediments in bodies of water while lower brominated molecules are more reactive and bind more easily to tissue, especially fat cells. When this was discovered in the 1990s and 2000s, lower brominated PBDEs began to be phased out, though higher brominated PBDEs are still in use. Though not safe, our world seems safer, saved from burning up while lowering our risk of toxicity.

But the stream flows on from our world to theirs, and higher brominated PBDEs do not stay put or stay themselves. Blowing in the wind; leaching through the underworld of a landfill after a torrential rain; sifting through the shafts of afternoon light refracting in the waters of a Minnesota lake; gyring on microplastics in the ocean; settling into the muck of a stream, pond, or continental shelf, higher brominated PBDEs have the potential to form great reservoirs in soils and sediments. All the world is a stream, and in that stream bacteria encounter these "safe(r)" molecules and biotransform them into lower brominated PBDEs, their bromine atoms stripped and danced off into some other eddy of the flow.

I was born into a PBDE world and I am thoroughly made by it, made through it, made of it. Who would I be without the bed I lie in, the TV I watch, the computer I'm tapping out these words on right now? I could have lived that other life and I think I could have been happy. PBDEs reduce the risks of injury by fire, but I could have lived a more careful life. PBDEs allow for intense electrical activity without combustion, but I could have lived a more measured life. PBDEs allow for automobiles, but I could have walked. PBDEs allow for toasters, but who needs toast? The eye, nose, tongue, body, and mind are burning with desire for safety, but at what cost? We fool ourselves when we think we are making our world safe(r) without recognizing that our world is also theirs, bacteria protozoa insect fish bird, and that their world is always and inevitably also ours.

I am awash in a great flood, and it frightens me. Eagles and I are not all that different. As apex predators, we both receive what the stream pours down our throats: television and cell phone and laptop casings, automobile upholstery and mattresses and curtains and carpets, wire sheathings and toaster ovens and video game consoles feasted on by bacteria feasted on by protozoa feasted on by insects feasted on by small fish feasted on by larger fish. The eagle and I both tear at salmon flesh and in the process feast on all of it that this world has to offer—this world that is burning because I am afraid to burn.

Foothill Yellow-legged Frog *(Rana boylii)*

WATER

—

Water makes up more than half of the body weight of all multicellular animals. Of that water, one-third bathes the cells, and the rest is held within them. Among vertebrates, the chemistry of that extra- and intracellular fluid is remarkably similar. The water within animals contains solutes (electrolytes such as calcium, chloride, sodium, and potassium; proteins such as albumin and globulin) that maintain the animal's fluid balance. To keep the water where it needs to be, all animals have excretory systems—kidneys and (in many cases) a bladder—that regulate the concentration of solutes. The kidneys work with the cardiovascular system to regulate blood pressure and rid the body of wastes like nitrogen and phosphorous.

Water, like air, is also a medium. To move through it requires a fair amount of energy and coordination; most aquatic animals have a streamlined body form and highly specialized waterproof skin (with feathers, fur, mucus, or scales). To live within it requires an internal anatomy that can withstand high pressure as well as nitrogen gas. For aquatic animals, water is everything.

All animals find ways to maintain their fluid balance whether in the air, on land, or in water. The amount of water an animal needs to drink depends on the environment in which it evolved: the moisture in its diet, the availability of freshwater or salt water, the air temperature, wind, and average humidity; rainfall; the amount of shade.

Camels, for instance, have unusually small red blood cells that are adaptations to desert life. These cells expand when the camel drinks water and rehydrates, and they contract as the animal loses hydration. Frogs and butterflies can dehydrate rapidly because of their small size and porous skin. Too much freshwater runoff after a flood can dilute the salinity of the water flowing over a coral reef. Too much standing water in a meadow or forest can lead to blooms of insects as well as drowned root systems.

—*Lucy Spelman*

Over 50 percent of all recognized turtle species are considered threatened on the International Union for Conservation of Nature's Red List of Threatened Species, making them among the most imperiled animal groups on Earth. Habitat degradation and overexploitation drive most of this imperilment, but many threats endanger turtles. The threat of plastic ingestion is well documented in all seven marine turtle species, with both lethal and sublethal effects reported. Marine turtles worldwide regularly ingest both macroplastics (>5 mm) and microplastics (<5 mm), spanning a wide range of plastic types.

FROM
"Plastic Ingestion by Freshwater Turtles:
A Review and Call to Action"

BY
Adam G. Clause, Aaron J. Celestian,
and Gregory B. Pauly

PUBLISHED IN
Scientific Reports 11 (March 2021)

Transferability of Turtles

—

TINA CANE

Who thankless   plastic pollution   spurns macro-love for turtles
Who loving   fresh imperiled   yearns micro-truth of turtles

To you   unbiased proxy   we give
an accounting   of the (im)permanence of turtles

Survey every field   as a stream of verified love
Favor every waterway   as victorious result

A strong representation of form
is meaningful prioritized turtles

A diamond in the rough   urgent carapace
A scarcity of love   disposable drinking cup

To be adored   assemblage is needed
To be saved   replication and accounting heeded

Who wild   animal   our prospective adoration
Who imperiled   universe   O turtles integration

"Amphibians are at risk of extirpation in rivers that are altered by dams, diversions, water abstraction, and channelization. Even in watercourses free of anthropogenic physical obstruction, amphibians face altered flow regimes as climate changes. Precipitation patterns are shifting; extreme droughts and floods are increasing in frequency and severity and may have negative effects on amphibians. As our annual breeding censuses over 25 years at Alameda Creek indicated, extended multi-year drought indeed caused a short-term population decline in the endangered foothill yellow-legged frog, but numbers rebounded post-drought. We also found in both of our systems that seasonal drought in fall coincided with peaks in the prevalence and intensity of infection by [the disease-causing pathogenic fungus *Batrachochytrium dendrobatidis*] due to shifts in habitat availability and use by different life stages."

FROM

"Seasonal Drought and Its Effects on Frog Population
Dynamics and Amphibian Disease in Intermittent Streams"

BY

Sarah J. Kupferberg, Hana Moidu, Andrea J. Adams,
Alessandro Catenazzi, Marcia Grefsrud, et al.

PUBLISHED IN

Ecohydrology 15, issue 5 (July 2022): 1–15

Exodus

—

BEN GOLDFARB

Nina found the first frog in the shower, between her feet, when she bent her head to rinse shampoo from the kelpy mass of her hair. The animal crouched in the rivulets that trickled down her calves and across the porcelain. She cradled it in her calloused hands, the creature as cool and damp as a stone pried from soil. She removed the toothbrushes, hers and Dan's, from the glass by the sink, set the frog in the glass, and poured in a splash of tap water. Then she toweled off, put on clean jeans, and brought the frog to dinner.

During the meal the frog sat quietly, bracketed on the table by Dan's beer and Toby's milk. It was a mottled clay-colored thing, stippled with bumps and ridges, slimmer-waisted than the toads Nina had seen around the ranch, almost elegant. It clambered onto its hind feet and pressed its forefingers against the lip of the glass, revealing moist yellow skin on its undercarriage and foot webbing. Toby squirmed in his chair and fished out his phone.

"No phones at the table, Tobe," Nina said.

"I want to see what he is," Toby said. "With the app."

"Okay, but just that," Nina said. Toby held up his phone and watched a pinwheel spin as an algorithm processed the animal. A few seconds passed.

"A foothill yellow-legged frog," Toby announced.

"Well, we're in the foothills and he's got yellow legs," Dan said. He spooned sour cream into his baked potato. "Makes sense."

"What should we do with him?" Toby said.

"I'm thinking we put him in Allan's stock pond," Nina said. "Usually some frogs in there."

After Toby cleared the dishes, Nina took the frog in its glass out to the 4Runner and they all drove down to Allan's. It was still light, a golden late-April evening, the brome on the hills pelt-soft. Allan rocked on his front porch and raised a beer in salutation. "Frog rescue mission," Toby called out the window, and Allan, who couldn't hear even at close range, shrugged and waved them through.

The stock pond, though, didn't hold a drop of water. The drought had shriveled it to a muddy pit crosshatched with the hoofprints of Allan's Black Angus. They climbed from the truck and Dan set down the glass. "Hop on out now," he said. The frog didn't move.

"He doesn't want to go," Toby said. "He needs water."

"Should rain soon," Dan said. They all looked at the cloudless peach sky.

"He'll die here," Toby said. "He'll dry up. Or get eaten."

"Don't need another pet," Dan said. "Your mom's got enough going on with the goats and the horses." He tipped the glass on its side and tapped the bottom. The frog bounded out and landed with a splat. Its amber irises sparked in the low light.

"See?" Dan said. "Happy as a pig."

*

The next batch of frogs turned up a week later, in the kitchen sink. Nina had filled it to the rim and slid in a crusty casserole dish to soak. When she came back after putting Toby to bed, three frogs were kicking through greasy dishwater. Nina corralled them with a mason jar, in which they piled atop each other like stones in a cairn.

"Probably coming up from the cellar," Dan said. He thumped down the wooden stairs to the basement, then thumped back up thirty minutes later, dirt-smudged and perturbed. "No cracks, holes, points of entry, anything like that," he said. "We got this place sealed up tight. I don't get it."

Nina was accustomed to sharing their ranch with wildlife—with the mule deer that stotted up the draws on spring-loaded legs, the gray foxes that barked raspily when she approached their den. The abundance of animals was one of the things she loved about the place; years ago, she'd even taken pre-reqs for vet school, before they had Toby and Dan talked her into minding the homestead full-time while he fit pipe. Yet the frogs unsettled her, owing, perhaps, to some deep-seated Sunday school association. Didn't the arrival of frogs augur trouble? One minute you're relocating a few amphibians, the next you're burying your firstborn.

Two mornings later, after the toilet refused to flush, Nina opened the tank and found it alive. Frogs writhed in such densities that they seemed a single mass. They flung themselves at the walls, clambered across the brick she'd stuck in the tank to save water. Nina set the lid back on, counted to ten, lifted it again. Still there. She remanded the frogs to a five-gallon bucket with an old aquarium net, tossed in the three from the jar, and drove them all to Allan's pond, where she released them. The frogs milled around uncertainly on the sunbaked mud, like commuters waiting for a train that might never come. Nina, observing the obvious unsuitability of this waterless plain for aquatic life, felt her chest clutch. She got back in the truck quickly and drove home.

*

Over the following weeks, the situation intensified. Frogs in Toby's bath, in the damp soil of houseplants, in the sink as Dan shaved. Nina stopped taking them to Allan's pond, which felt like a death sentence, but she wasn't sure what to do with them; all the nearby pools and streams were dry. She kept them in the bucket with an inch of water and fed them dead flies from the windowsills.

A biologist named Steve came over to offer his assessment. Nina knew him from an incident a few years earlier, when a mountain lion had killed one of their goats and she'd asked the state's fish and wildlife department to relocate the cat. The guy who answered the phone said the department tended to kill problem lions, so Nina made a few more calls and found Steve, who earned his living catching and tracking animals for research projects. Steve had captured the lion—haughty, graceful, impossibly powerful—in a metal cage his first night at Nina's place. The next morning he'd loosed the lion in the mountains, though he refused to tell Nina where; said that it would be safer for the cat if no human knew where he was; that even he, Steve, had forgotten where he'd freed the animal.

"Tough year for them yellow-legs," Steve said now as Nina and Toby led him down the basement stairs. "With the pools going dry. I seen some dead ones at Alameda Creek when I was up there catchin' bats last week."

"How do you catch a bat?" Toby asked.

"Toss 'em a fly on a line, same as a trout," Steve said. He turned back to wink at Toby, who narrowed his eyes skeptically.

"Been a good year for yellow-legs in our house," Nina said. She lifted the bucket's lid. Frogs popped against the wall like heated corn.

"Well, damn," Steve said. He absentmindedly rubbed the coyote tattoo that howled on his forearm. "You got yourselves a regular occupation. You said they was in the shower?"

"And the sink," Toby said.

"And the houseplants," said Nina. "What are they doing here?"

Steve spit on his hands, rubbed them together, and reached into the bucket to extract a frog. It perched on his upturned palm, its throat pulsing rhythmically, and Nina stifled an urge to reach out a finger and caress the soft, creamy membrane. "I'm thinking maybe it's the drought," Steve said. "In the wild, you know, you'll see 'em stacked up in any water they can find—little seep, spring, stock pond, whatever—until it dries up or they give each other the fungus disease and die. Now that all the natural water is gone, what are they doing?"

"Looking for it in the house," Toby said.

Steve nodded. "Bingo. When there ain't no spring, find a sink."

"What should we do about it?" Nina asked.

"Not sure you should do much of anything," Steve said. "Open a beer, maybe. Most people go their lives never seeing a yellow-legs. And here you got yourselves a frog sanctuary." He grinned at Toby and slipped the frog back into its bucket. "Oughta be proud."

That night Nina filled her sinks to the brim. The bathtub, too, and every pot, pan, and cupcake tin she could find. Into the living room came a battered old horse trough, an inflatable kiddie pool, a wheelbarrow. She filled them all. Dan looked at her like she was nuts, told her he wouldn't stand to have his house turned into a frog pit. Nina said she wasn't sure he had much choice. Toby clung to her legs as they argued. After Dan stalked off to bed, slamming the door behind him, Nina went to the basement, seized the bucket by its handle, and brought it upstairs. "Do the honors," she told Toby, who pried off the lid and—gently, gently—tipped it onto its side to let the frogs out.

*

December, now. Nina awakens before daybreak, inhales the musk of goats and the sweat of horses, and briefly experiences the same disorientation she's felt every morning for the last month: Where is she? The tickle of hay against her neck, the fridge-like hum of the farm cat who nuzzles her chest: right, yes, the barn. She frees an arm from her sleeping bag and touches Toby where he lies beside her, his narrow, bony back rising and falling in sleep. Dan is with his parents in Sacramento, where he's been staying since May.

She wriggles from the bag, shoves out the barn door, and crosses the hundred feet to the house, the dry grass brittle as broomstraw. Their house, when she steps into the mudroom, practically smothers her in its humid greenhouse breath, rank with the vegetal smell of the rotten bananas and pears she's left to attract flies, slugs, snails. She flicks the light switch and the ground itself seems to move—the subtle, trippy twitch of a shifting mosaic of small bodies, blanketing the floor in a layer as dense and soft as shag carpeting.

The first egg masses had appeared in the bathtub in mid-May, not long after Steve's visit: translucent clumps of nodules, firm-skinned and clustered as grapes. Before long the eggs had gained black spots, and one morning she awoke to find they'd all hatched, the tub a frenzy of tadpoles zooming back and forth. Steve told her not to clean the water—told her that the tadpoles would graze the algae, metamorphose into froglets, and, if she could keep them alive, hop off into the wilds come October, summoned back to their natural habitat by fall rains. But October had passed without a shower, and the frogs, now endowed with legs and lungs, had stayed put. Instead it was Nina and Toby who'd evacuated to the barn, giving the frogs the undisturbed run of the place.

Nina steps gingerly through the living room, each footfall carefully placed to avoid her guests. The frogs are as oddly silent as ever, hardly a croak or chirrup, though Nina could swear that sometimes they call *underwater,* wet bleats that rise from the tub like soap bubbles. She half-drains the bath and refills it, refreshes each pot and pan. She hears the hiss of pipes, the low murmur that is the song of dams and reservoirs and canals and conduits, the incomprehensibly vast infrastructure that appropriates water for the benefit of her own kind. She tops off the horse trough and turns off the lights on the way out, plunging the house back into its predawn gloom.

Common bottlenose dolphins, *Tursiops truncatus,* that inhabit brackish inshore estuaries have been observed in salinities ranging from 15 to 25 ppt. These inshore dolphins can suffer adverse health effects from prolonged freshwater exposure and pollution introduced from surface runoff, which can occur as a result of natural climatic events. For example, a high-precipitation event that coincided with local agricultural pesticide applications and reduced bay salinities to <10 ppt for several months was likely associated with a dolphin Unusual Mortality Event (UME), a period in which there is a significant die-off of a marine mammal population, along the mid-Texas coast. Poor water quality, prolonged freshwater exposure, and changes in water temperature were associated with increases in dolphin skin lesion prevalence and extent in multiple populations. Additionally, abrupt changes in water quality and salinity caused by floods were associated with the development of poxvirus-like skin lesions on Indo-Pacific bottlenose dolphins, *Tursiops aduncus.*

FROM

"Common Bottlenose Dolphin, *Tursiops truncatus,*
Behavioral Response to a Record-Breaking Flood Event
in Pensacola Bay, Florida"

BY

Shauna McBride-Kebert and Christina N. Toms

PUBLISHED IN

Journal of Zoological and Botanical Gardens 2 (2021): 351–69

Brackish

—

HESTER KAPLAN

She could sleep through her own weather events, whipping off the sheets and then grabbing them back a minute later, muttering somnolent swears. But he couldn't sleep through the night anymore, not with the burning planet of his wife next to him, not with her tidal waves and her shivering, not with the strange brackish smell she had begun to emit. Not that he would ever tell her any of this or that sometimes he felt he was witnessing the searing of what had once been a green and verdant garden he had played in.

He was pretty sure he had a half-blown sleep disorder by now, abetted by the poisonous blue-light from his laptop which he opened when he was awake like this in the middle of the night. He would not consider moving to another bed; it seemed right to share, as best he could, in her storms. Beyond the hill of his knees, he saw that it had begun to snow, much too early in October. He imagined opening the bedroom window and watching the fat flakes evaporate on the hot plain of his wife's bared flank.

If he let his finger wander at this indefinite hour, clicking on random links to videos and turning off the sound, it was amazing what he could fall into that would ease him back to sleep—the life cycle of the saguaro cactus, or a montage of imploding buildings. Tonight it was animals caught in floods: images of chickens hunkered on a tin roof, goats up to their necks in brown water, zoo creatures on the loose in a city he didn't recognize. And then dolphins, their pewter hides cratered with skin lesions, in a place he did recognize: Pensacola Bay, where his mother had owned a waterfront condo.

Last year, a month before she died, she had called him on the day when more rain fell there than in recorded history. There was fresh water where salt water was supposed to be, she'd said, salt water in the swimming pool, soaking her patio cushions. My sugar tastes like salt and my salt tastes like sugar. The inlet beyond her balcony had turned purple and metallic, and in the days following the deluge, she'd watched through her binoculars a solitary dolphin that swam in slower arcs of despair that he'd ever find his way again.

His mother had alerted wildlife management who told her they were already on top of the problem. When they finally showed up, they couldn't find the animal, though they assured her that it had survived, that it had just been disoriented by the weather and its search for the bay's right salinity level. His mother wasn't convinced, but she'd never been an optimist.

He closed his computer abruptly, puzzled by where tonight had led him—to his dead mother and bewildered wildlife afraid of drowning. What had happened to that dolphin? And his mother? Where had they gone?

"Huh," his wife said, and went into the bathroom.

What had happened to her, this woman he'd been married to for decades? Who was she now, full in the cascade of her life?

He heard her pee: she was a stream, a waterfall in the dark. She got back into bed, a cool breeze. She was an aviary: there are tiny birds in my stomach, she said. She was a meteorologist: oh, look, it's snowing, she said, her eyes closed. She was a philosopher of the future, her feet kicking at the blankets. "It won't be long before the squirrels tip off their branches and wild pigs take over the park where our babies played. But then," she added, turning on her side, already mostly asleep, "but then, our babies will have babies floating in their own saline seas, and the storm will pass and you and I will still be here."

She reached behind herself to touch him. His phone on the bedside table pulsed with news from beyond. He thought of his three daughters in other cities. The motion sensor light on their neighbor's garage caught an intruder in its harsh beam and didn't let go. The snow's luminescence fell on his wife's skin, turning it silver, polished, mostly liquid, each pore in shadow. He kissed a drop of sweat that rolled down her forearm. It was salty and sweet. She was wiser than he was, and many steps ahead of him. He felt revived, but unlikely to sleep anytime soon. My wife, he whispered, is a dolphin.

The Boreal Toad (*Anaxyrus boreas boreas*) has declined throughout the southern Rocky Mountains and is listed as an endangered, or tier 1, species in Colorado, Wyoming, and New Mexico. Regional declines are primarily attributed to chytridiomycosis, a disease caused by the fungal pathogen *Batrachochytrium dendrobatidis*; however, some populations have declined despite low prevalence of the pathogen. One such population is in Spruce Lake in Rocky Mountain National Park, where a small population of Boreal Toads is declining despite high adult survival. Eggs are deposited at the site in most years, but recruitment into the adult breeding population is low, indicating low survival of the aquatic or subadult life stages. One hypothesis for the low recruitment is potential impacts of introduced Greenback Cutthroat Trout (*Oncorhynchus clarki stomias*), a listed subspecies under the Endangered Species Act, on Boreal Toad aquatic life stages. In 1991, Cutthroat Trout, believed to be greenbacks, were introduced to Spruce Lake, which was historically fishless. Bufonid eggs and tadpoles contain bufotoxins, making them unpalatable to many vertebrate predators, including trout; however, laboratory studies suggest that trout frequently attempted to ingest toad tadpoles, reducing tadpole survival probabilities. Trout affect tadpole survival in other amphibians by altering trophic interactions (e.g., by reducing the populations of aquatic insects) or by reducing the amount of time that tadpoles spend in resource-rich areas.

FROM

"Few Impacts of Introduced Cutthroat Trout (*Oncorhynchus clarki*) on Aquatic Stages of Boreal Toads (*Anaxyrus boreas boreas*)"

BY

John G. Crockett, Wendy E. Lanier, and Larissa L. Bailey

PUBLISHED IN

Journal of Herpetology 55, issue 3 (2021): 310–17

Where One Thing Begins

—

DAVID NAIMON

*The shell is a living fossil, like a fairy tale. Like a fairy tale,
it's an ancient casing that once held a breathing thing in
place. A similar spiral is encrypted in the inner ear and
hurricanes and spiderwebs and the uterus. It is proof of
where a story once lived or tried to live, and marked by the
same elliptical orbit that makes it practically impossible to
tell where one thing begins and where it ends.*
        —Sabrina Orah Mark, "The Silence of Witches"

Cutthroat trout listen with their entire bodies. The same density as water,
they have no need for an outer ear. Not even an ear opening. Sound passes
right through their bodies, bodies that vibrate with the wave of sound.
Sound that arrives at their inner ear from their vibrating bodies.

The smallest bones in the human body—the incus, stapes, and hammer—
the three tiny ossicles in our middle ear, are often what paleontologists
use to classify fossils as mammalian, to distinguish us from others unlike
us. But much of how we hear, how we listen, comes from sea creatures,
from the sea. The ear canal from fish, and the middle ear dreamed into
being by amphibians, an architecture created by creatures wanting to
hear sound both in air and in water.

When we hold a seashell to our ears it is not the ocean we are hearing.
Rather the spiral shell, the one deep within our heads, the cochlea, and
the one now held in our hands, up in the air, against our heads, against
the shell-like whorl of cartilaginous flesh we colloquially call an "ear,"
these two shells together are remembering their origins, speaking fondly
of the shared water they've been lifted from.

Take the boreal toad and the fleshy circle drawn just behind its eyes, pulled taut like a rubbery drum. This is not baroque design—not only, but a tympanum, an eardrum, and behind it a middle ear much like ours, conducting sound from air. In true amphibian style, frogs and toads also hear in other ways, bodily. Some hear with their lungs, lungs that vibrate so well, that conduct their vibrations so ably to the inner ear that they spare the outer ear drum sonic stress. Others conduct sound to the ear through their mouths.

Listening through their mouths.

Through the ages many substances have been used to try to repair a perforated human ear drum—petroleum jelly, glycerine, water and saliva as adhesives to affix anything and everything: India rubber, lint, tin, silver foil, or the vitelline membrane of an egg to the rupture. But the first recorded attempts to repair our ability to listen were mediated by animals—a tube made of elk hoof connected to a pig's bladder to create a prosthetic drum.

The song of the boreal toad when it sings has been described by human ears as sounding like the peeping of a chick, and a chorus of boreal toads like a distant flock of Canadian geese. Toad sounds, flying through the air from toad to toad, from toad drum to toad drum, from toad lung to toad lung, from a singing toad mouth to a listening one, are known to be imitated by several species of bird.

In "Telling Is Listening" Ursula K. Le Guin writes: "Listening is not a reaction, it is a connection." "Everything said—is shaped as it is spoken by actual or anticipated response." "Speech connects us so immediately and vitally because it is a physical, bodily process, to begin with." "All living beings are oscillators. We vibrate. Amoeba or human, we pulse."

All vertebrate animals—trout, toad, and human alike—use hair cell bundles to sense their environments. Human hair cell bundles have turned inward, become hermetic, clustering deep within the spiral of the cochlear shell, nesting far from the exterior world and its creatures. When the roughly fifteen thousand hair cells hidden there, cells that translate and deliver signals to our brains, are damaged, the hearing loss that results is often irreparable.

Sea anemone and human hair cell bundles look remarkably alike, a correspondence that intrigues human scientists because, unlike us, sea anemones can repair them quickly and easily. Sea anemone hair cells are on the outside. Covering their tentacles, they are used as radar. When prey activate a tentacular hair cell bundle, the sea anemone releases, at a rate of acceleration five million times greater than that of gravity, a poisoned dart. Hair cell bundle damage occurs all the time in the course of daily sea anemone life, even when they reproduce, tearing themselves in two, and before you know it as good as new.

The hair cell bundles of the cutthroat trout also cover the exterior of their bodies, running laterally from gill to tail as part of the lateral line organ just under the skin. This system of sensory organs orients them to the direction and speed of water and helps them detect water's displacement by predators and prey. These outward-facing bundled and hairy cells are essential for a fish's ability to school and swim in unison.

Boreal toads are the only alpine toad in Colorado. The greenback cutthroat trout is Colorado's state fish. The boreal toad was once so numerous you'd see them dining on bugs beneath streetlamps in high-altitude Colorado towns. Today there are as few as eight hundred adult boreal toads left in the entire state. The greenback cutthroat trout has existed in the region for between three and five million years. In the 1930s Colorado's state fish was declared extinct. Decades later, small populations were discovered in remote pockets of the state. Cutthroat trout are considered one of the most beautiful North American fish. No one remarks on the beauty of a boreal toad. But because the boreal toad breathes through its skin, the collapse of its population is considered a bellwether, a canary in the coal mine, for the status of alpine wetlands. The greenback cutthroat trout, one of the continent's most endangered fish, requires water that is cold and clear. Cold, clear, and unobstructed. The toads concur.

Some humans study whether these two ailing species can be introduced into the same (warming and obstructed) water system, and ask whether the boreal toad and its bufotoxins taste bad enough not to be eaten by the trout, and would like to find wild sanctuaries for both toad and trout to recover, and have tentatively concluded that the toad and the trout can and would like to coexist together in the same ecosystem, and seem to be making a gesture of attentive listening in the desire to repair and restore, and yet . . .

      . . . "it matters what matters we use to think other matters with" says anthropologist Donna Haraway. "What knots knot knots, what thoughts think thoughts."

Once upon a time, a time when scientists pursued knowledge also through art-making, an ebb and flow between feeling and thought, a time of poet-naturalists, a particular poet-naturalist who might've been named Franz or Bruno, Italo or Aldo, Wangari, Karthika, or Jalal, but who, for our purposes was named Clarice (though some called her Clara, and others Cécile), placed her thick-fingered hand in the water before she studied it—the water, the water and its inhabitants, the hand, the human hand, hers, the hand through and in the water. Clarice: studying and studied. A study as shell, a hand within the shell, a hand shaped by the shell, a hand shelling the shell it is shaped by.

Approaching the lake, cold and clear, too cold for a human hand, but not cold and clear enough for others, Clarice clapped in the air, a sound that struck the drum of the boreal toads, unseen. A sound that struck her drums as well. A sound they shared. She knelt at the lake's edge, one knee on the frozen mud, patted her pocketed book of sketch and lyric and note, removed her glasses so each and every thing she saw blurred just a little, one to the next, edges fuzzed just enough so it was practically impossible to tell where one thing began and another . . .

She broke the water's surface with a hand, her non-dominant right, and let the water assume the shape of it, let her hand displace a hand-shaped space in the water. She looked at her submerged hand from the air. It too wavering, its edges unstable in the water-refracted light, its position not quite aligned with her arm above the water, but in a different space, in the shell of the study, where its coldness, the pain of its coldness, seemed like a pain of the lake. Not not of the hand, but not not of the lake.

Clarice knew the trout would sense the displacement of the water by her hand, that they would hear that displacement with their bodies. She knew the toads would too. From above the water she knew there were things she could never know, and in that not-knowing she moved her intelligence into her hand below. She moved her intelligence into her hand and opened her mouth. She opened her mouth not to make a noise but to listen.

Clarice unfixed her eyes while her hand grew colder and colder still. Her hand increasingly felt like something "other," and yet her attention increasingly gathered there. She could feel the cold alpine air pinch at the back of her pharynx. The sound of her breathing, from the exertion of her stillness, was something she could not help; its sound was part of her, its sound part of her listening to the place she was part of.

Yet another sound, one that began far below her fingers, or so she imagined, as if she were the smallest part, the tiniest bone, deep within the spiral folds of a large unseen ear, a whorl whose three ossicles distinct, one to the next—toad, trout, human—sounded together a sound from none and all of them, vibrating her hand, pulsing her throat, an unknown sound passing up and out of her.

A flock of Canadian geese flying far above seemed to come closer, to fly lower, to take note of the note sounded, to study the sound and its origins, to nod to the lake and its inhabitants, an affirmative nod, a *yes*, as if to say, "us too," without ever breaking formation, before finding a new draft, a spiral staircase of air, rising, turning, and departing. And sounding in that draft, more and more in the distance, like a chorus of toads.

Critical habitat for giant gartersnakes, while formally undefined, is inextricably linked to water supply, distribution, and application across the Central Valley landscape. Limitations to water on the landscape related to water supply, cropping patterns, or wetland restoration can have large effects on giant gartersnake populations. The challenge in managing water for giant gartersnakes is like that for other water management issues in California, including increasing variability in precipitation patterns and generally increasing demand for water for a variety of uses.

FROM
"A Tale of Two Valleys: Endangered Species Policy and the Fate of the Giant Gartersnake"

BY
Brian J. Halstead, Patricia Valcarcel, Richard Kim, Anna C. Jordan, Jonathan P. Rose, et al.

PUBLISHED IN
California Fish and Wildlife Journal 107 (July 2021): 264–83

On Comedy Night, the Giant Gartersnake Fails at Open Mic

—

ALBERTO RÍOS

1.

I look in the mirror of everywhere,
  But cannot see myself.

I drink at the well of everything,
  But the well itself is dry.

My last name is snake, and my family is large.
  I have cousins but they've moved on.

You and I, we know each other well—
  You are scared of me. I am scared of you.

I am a water pipe, a wormhole, a fence post,
  A drug smuggler's tunnel under a heavy wall.

I am the vein in a coyote's leg.
  A pea-shooter, a flagpole, a kite tail.

I am all over the alphabet and numbers,
  The numeral 1, and of course the capital S.

I am the hanging bell chime in a philharmonic orchestra.
  I am a straw.

2.

All this in strange dreams. They say it is lack of water,
And that may be true—I can't find my cousins anymore.

No water may mean no us. No water also means
No rice. So much *no* to so many things.

Curiously, too much water is no better.
We are reduced finally to fairy tales:

We choose the third option, the *something-just-right*.
It is a Goldilocks world of gymnastic balance.

In the middle, just right and as good neighbors, we live—
Happy, content, thriving on an elegant adequacy.

A little more or a little less and the scale is tipped.
The world is not our place anymore.

I will be a mother. I will be a father.
I will give my water even if I go without. World,

You are my bully. Half friend, half enemy, protector,
Destroyer. Tomorrow the sun rises. May we be here.

Coral populations have declined globally in the past three decades. Two acroporid species, *Acropora cervicornis* and *Acropora palmata,* which previously dominated the Caribbean, and were major reef builders through millennia, have experienced some of the largest declines. Diseases and thermal anomalies have been the main causes of coral population declines in the Caribbean. A major outbreak of white-band disease in the 1970s caused a 95 percent decline in Caribbean acroporids. Since then, *A. cervicornis* and *A. palmata* have been listed as 'threatened' under the US Endangered Species Act in 2006 and 'critically endangered' on the World Conservation Union (IUCN) Red List in 2008. Coral restoration efforts are now attempting to restore acroporid populations along the Florida reef tract. . . . However, restoration through propagation and outplanting techniques alone will not be enough if the benchmarks set by the Paris Agreement are not met.

FROM

"Ranking 67 Florida Reefs for Survival of
Acropora cervicornis Outplants"

BY

Raymond B. Banister and Robert van Woesik

PUBLISHED IN

Frontiers in Marine Science 8 (July 2021): 1–10

Three Sonnets without a Barrier Reef

—

CRAIG SANTOS PEREZ

1.

I hold my wife's hand during the ultrasound.
"That's your future," the doctor says, pointing
to a fetus floating in amniotic fluid.
One night a year, after the full moon, after the tide
touches a certain height, after the water reaches
the right temperature, only then will the ocean
cue swollen coral polyps to spawn, in synchrony,
a galaxy of gametes. These buoyant stars dance
to the surface, open, fertilize, and form larvae.
Some are eaten by plankton and fish, others sink
to substrate or seabed, where they root and bud.
We listen to our unborn daughter's heartbeats.
"She looks like a breathing island,"
my wife says, whose body is a barrier reef.

2.

The weather spawns another hurricane above Hawai'i.
Rain drums the pavement as flood warning alerts
vibrate our cellphones. In bed, we read a children's book,
The Great Barrier Reef, to our daughter,
who's two years old now, snuggled between us.
"The corals have mouths, stomachs, and arms,"
we tell her, pointing to our matching body parts.

"They form families, like us. They even build homes
and villages." She loves every colorful picture
of tropical fish and intricate corals; I love
that the pictures never change. We close the book,
kiss her forehead, and whisper: "Sweet dreams."
She is our most vulnerable island,
and we are her barrier reef.

3.

In my dream, we are swimming at the beach.
The shore is eroded. The ocean is warm
and murky. The waves are strong and rising.
No fish, anywhere. Our daughter points
to what looks like bleached and broken skeletons
and asks, "Daddy, are the corals dead?"
I don't tell her about thermal stress, diseases,
or pollution. I don't tell her about corals
struggling to spawn, frozen in vaults, reared
in nurseries, and outplanted by scientists.
"Don't worry," I say. "They're just sleeping."
She looks into the water and whispers:
"Sweet dreams." I hold her hand as the sun
sets without a barrier reef.

Freshwater aquatic systems are becoming increasingly degraded by anthropogenic activities including pollution, damming, water removal, overgrazing and overharvest of timber in surrounding catchments, land use change, invasive species, and climate change. To restore and protect streams and riparian areas, which are among the most imperiled ecosystems, environmental managers in some northern temperate regions are increasingly turning to management options involving North American beavers *(Castor canadensis)* or Eurasian beavers *(Castor fiber)*. Both species are ecosystem engineers that exert strong community and ecosystem-level effects at multiple spatial scales, primarily through dam-building.

FROM

"Beaver Dams Are Associated with Enhanced Amphibian Diversity via Lengthened Hydroperiods and Increased Representation of Slow-Developing Species"

BY

John M. Romansic, Nicolette L. Nelson, Kevan B. Moffett, and Jonah Piovia-Scott

PUBLISHED IN

Freshwater Biology 66, issue 3 (March 2021): 481–94

Keystone Species

—

SHARMA SHIELDS

After my cousin—age twelve to my age five—did what he did to me, an act I didn't understand and wouldn't understand for another four decades until he was arrested, put on trial, and finally sentenced to prison for harming other children, I staggered from the dim bedroom with its plaid pastel sheets and shelves of *Choose Your Own Adventures* and flowed ghostlike down the hallway, avoiding the adults drinking gin in my aunt's living room, shrinking from the family room where my brother and other cousins battled at an Atari, and pushed open the sliding glass doors of the den so I could slip into the damp forest with its weeping pine branches and smoking dragon of fog. It was early evening in early winter, on the verge of the deep freeze, and beneath my sneakers the ground crunched like small bones. There was already a spreading numbness in me like a knife to the stomach, a wound I could sense but that brought me no present pain. Forest-cradled, I carved through the trees to the river and flickered at its broad frozen edge not wanting to drown but to survive. I'd emerged from something incomprehensible to me, but I didn't yet know what incomprehensibility meant, and at this moment, too young yet to read or write well, too young to narrate myself into existence, I merely stood on the bank of the misty river and breathed. I was a living creature. No more and no less.

Another creature stirred then, water-born, round face and long body only slightly visible above the cold water. The creature was deep brown, almost black in the waning light, but with shining, lively dark eyes. The rivulets of the quiet pond formed a flowing cape behind the animal as they swam.

I'd seen the beavers here only once before, another of my earliest memories, but I didn't rejoice this time at their appearance, I only knelt and watched them curiously, the ice and wet earth spilling into my sneakers, the knees of my trousers now soggy. "Hello," I said, and my own voice was foreign to me. It was the first word I'd spoken in an hour or more, and it landed hard, causing the animal to flinch. I held out my hand as I'd been told to do with strange dogs, and the beaver swam fluidly forward but then stopped, the large rodent head swiveling one way and then the other.

"Alice," the beaver said, and how the creature knew my name remains a mystery to me. "Come with me."

The beaver's voice was rich and warm—kind. But, I reasoned, my cousin had also been kind. *Come with me. I'll show you my room. I'll read books to you.* How excited I'd been; how willing. His eyes had shone, too. He was already, even so young, learning to lure.

"For what?" I asked the beaver.

"Come swim with me. I'll show you our home."

I hesitated. It wasn't that the water was cold. It was that I was already telling myself the world wasn't safe, that no one could be trusted.

The beaver regarded me with black, feeling eyes for a long moment. "There is destruction and ruin, Alice. There is harm done to numerous bodies, animal and otherwise. I know you've seen it. You'll see more, too. Not just in your small life but all around us. But there are other parties who seek a gentler existence, who want to create, repair, soothe. These parties are not interested in entitlement, in the fruition of their desire or need to control. I want to show you."

Another beaver emerged from the water, swimming playfully, and behind this larger beaver was a smaller one, a younger beaver, and this is what drew me into the water, how healthy this youth seemed, how immediately obvious it was that there was care here, attention. Even then, even as mystified as I was by the beaver's words, confused by language and existence and behavior, I sensed a glowing truth: a family, a society, is only as healthy as its children feel safe.

These beavers, I could see, were a healthy family.

I moved into the water bravely, not even knowing how to properly swim. The two larger beavers nestled one under each of my armpits, their glistening bodies thick and muscular and confident, and, in this way, they guided me into the river. The young beaver followed us, playfully diving and surfacing. I found I could breathe underwater as well as I could breathe above it. Submerged, the world grayed and atomized, as though we floated not through water but through a dense particulate fog. We approached their home, the high lodge behind the dam, the elaborate architecture comprised of alder and willow, poplar and aspen, shirred cottonwood. The bare stripped branches reminded me of elven staffs, skillfully whittled, maybe even enchanted. This was a fairy world to me, and I forgot my numbness and gave myself over to its magic.

We passed their food store and pushed into the entrance, a tunnel I could barely squeeze through that ran uphill into the living area of the lodge. Here in the lodge's interior I was deposited, blinking and dripping, the only light coming through a ventilation shaft in the structure's ceiling. The beavers shook themselves dry and attended to me, making sure I wasn't too wet or too cold, the youngest of them, perhaps a year old or so, pushing against me as if to dry me off with their luxurious fur. I was cozy and comfortable and safe in this strange womb, the sound of water all around us, the creaking of the wood, the smell of damp earth and shorn sticks, the peaceful white noise of the pond. An exhaustion came over me, an awareness of what I had just endured, remembering my aunt's large ample house in the foothills of the Cascades where my family continued to vacation together, unperturbed and unaware of my new shakier existence. I was glad I was here and not there.

"The sound of the water impels us to dam," one of the older beavers told me, inviting me with her nose to sit. I did so, cross-legged, listening carefully. "The sound of the river brought us here, and we dammed it, and things began to change. The red-legged frogs reappeared. The northwestern and long-toed salamanders. The rough-skinned newts. We provided habitat for them, cleaner water, deeper water, still water. We slowed life down so life can take its time and flourish. And it's here we love our children. We work hard. We play. You will be told again and again that the history of life is brutal and cruel, that there are forces on our planet hellbent on harm, on control, but we want you to know, Alice, there are so many other forces here, too. There are hardworking forces whose efforts promote healing and good ancestry. There are forces benefitting more than just the self."

My younger self listened closely, but of course I understood very little of it at that age, only knew that what was being said to me was hope-infused, life-infused, an urgent plea to remember the good. I would tuck this experience like a pearl into the fabric of my existence, where it would glow unseen until I uncovered it years later in the therapist's office, surprised by its unmarred goodness as I picked apart the other more painful memories—finally—in an attempt to understand and grow past them. What a source of light this provided me, this winter evening spent with the American beavers.

Now, remembering this in my middle age, I think about what I want from my own life, the ability to create something meaningful, the chance to love fully and well, the opportunity to be a good ancestor in the short life we are given, to leave something beautiful and considerate behind, to foment in my own way healthy relationships with the community around me. I'm thrilled at how like storytelling the beaver dam and lodge are, constructed by these meticulously carved and arranged materials—shards of memories, the twigs, rocks, and mud of our complex lives—and how the beavers are constant even after being hunted, hurt, decimated themselves. How they've returned to our wetlands to help, despite it all. How they haven't succumbed to the hurt, haven't decided to wage it like a cudgel against others, as so many hurt beings do. How they heal, how they heal, how they heal. How their hard work is like endless love. As a child, their words moved me, but I didn't yet understand them. There was so much I didn't understand. But the gift was planted to return to later, and for that I'm grateful.

Now when the beavers told my young self that they had to return me to the edge of the pond, I stiffened and shook my head. I wanted to stay with them. I couldn't imagine returning to my aunt's house. How would

I move through those rooms where I had been harmed, fearful of what else might happen to the bodies of the world's children?

"Take heart, Alice," the largest beaver told me. "Remember what we told you about the forces for good. Seek them out. Forge peace how you can. Work hard at what you love. When you break down, find help. There will come a time when you can no longer hide from that which has hurt you—there will be voices telling you, wrongly, that you deserve the hurt. You will need to swim upstream. It will take you a long time to heal. Good things take a long time. They take work. Build your dam. Love your community. Make a home in the deep, clean, still water."

The words rushed into me and hid in their small, hard, concentrate form deep within my viscera. The beavers drew me back through the tunnel, across the pond, onto the shoreline with its thickening ice. I couldn't yet see but could imagine my aunt's house with its big illumined windows, all of its lights ignited as though its interior were set on fire. I said goodbye to the generous beavers and thanked them, and then, the coldness of the water finally occurring to me, the spell of the beavers broken, I moved stiffly up the pathway to the house, already telling myself, *Nothing has happened, it was no big deal, I don't matter, anyway,* my method of surviving for the next four decades. But with this numbness was also a future resolve: *There is goodness in the world, and maybe, one day, even in me. I'll find it and cultivate it,* this new thought the smallest of seedlings uncurling.

And somewhere nearby, gathering in the teeming pools they are always creating, the beavers have returned to their life-saving work.

Jaguar *(Panthera onca)*

SHELTER

—

Burrow. Cave. Den. House. Nest. Rock. Tree. Among the many words we use for "shelter," all imply the same thing: a protected, safe place. For some animals, a shelter provides protection from extreme weather or predators. For others, it ensures the immediate environment is just right in terms of temperature, humidity, light, food, and access to a mate.

Most animals find shelter within the larger spaces (habitats or ecosystems) where they live: a shady tree branch for a jaguar or a hollow tree cavity for a bat. Some animals make their own home again and again: pika dig holes, beavers build dens (and leave them empty for otters), and some birds make new nests in the same tree each year. Foxes, rabbits, and rats often share the same hole, if at different times. Migrating animals find or create shelter along their route. Humans make the most elaborate homes, and in the process destroy those of others. Many of us purposefully do all we can to keep other creatures out. Yet our houses, office buildings, and related structures (attics, basements, chimneys, gutters, sewers, and so on) create enticing new habitats for all kinds of animals, especially those we are not too keen on encountering: bedbugs, dust mites, mice, rats, and sugar ants, for example.

How we arrange the land around our homes, towns, cities, and roads creates new and altered habitats, as does everything we put into these spaces, such as shrubs for ground cover, fast-growing trees for shade, and flowering plants for color. This new-ish arrangement can be positive, neutral, or negative. The animals seem to go for it, having no way of knowing that many people react badly (irrationally or not) when they suddenly meet up with a fox or a yellow jacket or find themselves dodging pigeon poop from above.

At the same time, many of us are pleasantly surprised to find red-tailed hawks, owls, and other birds of prey in our cities; fish, frogs, and waterfowl in our artificial ponds and pools; songbirds in our backyards; and, where we plant for pollinators, bees and butterflies in our highway medians. Even the occasional sighting of a black bear or bobcat can be thrilling.

—*Lucy Spelman*

Several bat species in North America have recently experienced severe population declines due to a fungal pathogen introduced from Eurasia, *Pseudogymnoascus destructans,* which causes white-nose syndrome. The fungus infects bats and grows into their epidermal tissue during hibernation, when bats cool their bodies down to near ambient hibernaculum temperatures. Ambient temperatures vary within and among hibernacula, and bats in eastern North America roost between 7°C and 11°C on average, depending on the bat species. Individual bats can select microclimates that optimize temperature-dependent energy use with other physiological constraints during hibernation, and over the range of temperatures used by bats, the fungus has nonlinear, temperature-dependent growth in vitro. In particular, the fungus grows optimally near 12–16°C on growth media, with a thermal range between 0°C and ~21°C. Fungal loads on bat wings are strongly correlated with damage to wing tissue and population impacts. Therefore, we hypothesized that the invasion of *P. destructans* would alter thermal habitat suitability for bats, where warmer roosts would have higher fungal growth and bat mortality, and bats might alter their microclimate preferences across hibernacula from pre-invasion to post-invasion in response to this selection pressure.

FROM

"Continued Preference for Suboptimal Habitat
Reduces Bat Survival with White-nose Syndrome"

BY

Skylar R. Hopkins, Joseph R. Hoyt, J. Paul White,
Heather M. Kaarakka, Jennifer A. Redell, et al.

PUBLISHED IN

Nature Communications 12, number 166 (2021)

Mammalian

—

DAVID BAKER

1.

Stubborn. That's one thing.
The little brown bat,
 whom scholars call *Myotis lucifugus,*

will not be moved to
leave its habitat,
 so is dying now in drastic numbers.

A culprit pathogen,
which causes white-
 nose syndrome, multiplies their "fungal load"

by spreading through the
bats' epidermal
 tissue during hibernation. To wit:

the virus *Pseudo-*
gymnoascus
 destructans—can you believe that?—traced

from Eurasia to
New York, through the Midwest,
 just since 2006. It's invasive

as kudzu or
capitalism. It
    infects the established hibernacula

of the little bats,
who won't abandon
    their nesting grounds. Such places the scholars

agree are "suboptimal habitat."

2.

Ours was high in a shadow of rafters.
My father swept it, lightly, with a towel
—1960-something—so I carried it
loose in a pillowcase to the basement,
to the aquarium we packed with twigs,
damp grass, a little pie-tin to drink from,
its long wings "very much like a human
arm and hand," its tan skin taut as suede pulled
across a fine branching of bone. All day

it would not eat. What could it see? Echo
and sorrow—I mean ours—though we tried eye-
droppers of egg, houseflies dropped in. We tried
to apologize with care. Delicate
tipped folds of its ears, mouse fur, but one wing
awry, like a twig snapped, useless. They lack,
said our book, "eyeshine," though little brown bats
can be distinguished by hairs on their feet
that extend beyond the length of their toes.

3.

Maybe memory
isn't a science
    but like science is a way of knowing.

The bats stay true to
their known refugia—
    problem is, per one study, they "continue

to select habitats
where *P. destructans*
    severity is highest." Such sites become,

scholars tell us, "e-
cological traps."
    The data's undeniable: where pre-

and post-invasion
comparisons show
    a "distribution shift analysis . . .

a large proportion
[52%] still
    used relatively warm roosts." They won't, that

is, be moved—though
"fungal loads increase
    with early hibernation roosting

temperatures." The instinct to stay's too strong.

4.

The last I saw was last month, the last light
over the windward islands, like a wing.
We were in love again. We sat in the glow
of stars alive or long dead. Suddenly
they were with us, skittering just above
our bay balcony. The bare wind with wings.
Sipping mosquitoes. Unmistakable
their flight lines, jagged as constellations.
Fruit or free-tailed, an island cousin, up

from the inward caves or scrub woods. Peepers
called then, and doves; a cargo ship passed
slowly out of sight. We apologized
for what we had done. Stubborn. I mean us.
And the other thing. There are so many
—bobcat and vole, killer whale, bonobo—
in the vast taxonomy of mammalia.
Yet these remain the only ones of all
able to
                —of course, ours never would—fly.

New England cottontails are reluctant to forgo dense understory cover, which provides both food and refuge. Within patches of shrubland ≤ 2.5 hectares, New England cottontails engage in atypical behavior for the species, foraging further from cover, and experience reduced winter survival when compared to patches ≥ 5 hectares. This observation, coupled with low abundance within these patches, indicates small patches may act as population sinks; however a formal study of space use in relation to patch size has not been undertaken. Furthermore, although seasonal differences in environmental productivity and habitat availability often result in differences in space use, studies of New England cottontails and the conservation strategies developed from these studies have overwhelmingly focused on the winter, when survival is presumed lowest. Resource scarcity, such as the availability of cover or soft mast, during spring and summer combined with the onset of reproduction during this time are suspected to limit populations of other small mammals in seasonal environments. . . . Given that reproductive output is also a better indicator of population growth than adult survival in other short lived rabbits, consideration of the summer space needs of New England cottontails may be critical for developing strategies focused on population recovery.

FROM

"Determinants of Home-range Size of Imperiled
New England Cottontails *(Sylvilagus transitionalis)* and
Introduced Eastern Cottontails *(Sylvilagus floridanus)*"

BY

Amanda E. Cheeseman, Jonathan B. Cohen, Sadie J. Ryan,
and Christopher M. Whipps

PUBLISHED IN

Canadian Journal of Zoology 97 (June 2019): 516–23

Johnny Cottontail

—

AIMEE BENDER

My father, who hates rabbits, feels bad for these. He sees them hop out, exposed, between shrubs. Little bunny ears, little trembling bunny body, visible between the blueberry and the multiflora rosa, between the Japanese barberry and the Oriental bittersweet. He used to shoot them and skin and eat them when he was a boy in Kentucky—on a spit, even!—but he has lost the taste for rabbit, and now when he sees them out in the open he too much relates, he who cannot walk on his own anymore, he who is feeble; "they are feeble, too," he says, over breakfast. "Who the fuck thought I would relate to a rabbit? Old age makes all the idiots into friends."

My house, where he is now, after having been transported almost overnight once his wife—my stepmother—died from a rapid cancer, is where he'll stay. It felt like he'd airdropped through the ceiling, how he landed inside the guest-room bed and in the morning was suddenly sitting there at the breakfast table like a figment from my childhood, eyebrows raised. "Everything has changed," he said, accepting a bowl of cereal, "why not make everything change more? Coffee?" He has a low gravelly voice that used to scare me as a child but now reminds me of thunder in the distance, a promise of rain. Our home butts at the edge of a couple of former agricultural lots sold to private buyers, still overgrown with shrubs which have spread over the land and form—or used to form—a cover for the bunnies, the New England cottontail, the type the children love, that Farmer MacGregor despised. "I used to *be* Farmer MacGregor," says Dad, grumbling into his mug. "Now I'm Johnny Cottontail or whatever." He hates the walker. He stumbles through the rooms without it but the walls already have scratch marks where his fingernails scrape. We tell him he should use it, he might fall, he might break a hip and that's it, that's the end, but he says who cares, all routes lead to the same end, maybe a hip is the way to go, is the proper doorway. It's probably grief speaking, but not just for her: for his mobility, his ease. Also, he says it like this now, before he's in a hospital with a broken hip, wasting away.

Our picture window looks out on these shrubs but the new home-owners—the Wingfields—who bought the property last year have started to landscape and cut back and the patches have fragmented into leafy blobs framed by lakes of open land, of dirt, which is why we see the bunnies poking through and hopping between one and the other, shelter to shelter, bush to bush. My daughter swears she saw one swept up by a hawk, inside the hawk's talons, but I don't know if it's even possible. She wants a bunny as a pet. Dad says they're dumb pets. "They just sit there and their nose goes up and down," he says, settling onto the couch to look out the window. "Get a dog." I put out a few carrot shavings as a lure and they're gone by morning. He tried to take me hunting once but I cried the whole time.

"The barberry are invasive," says Dad, gesturing at the scene. Another gray bunny visible, dashing into the bushes. They're like people crossing the street in New York City, frightened of a bus. "Taking over. Shrubbing up everything." He just read an article. He told my daughter a dog could round up the bunnies, but she's allergic to fur. We can't get a bunny either but maybe she could pretend to own one outside, could mark a specific special rabbit friend with her eyes.

My daughter is not afraid of my father, and he is not especially fond or not fond of her, but they do like to sit side by side on that couch and look out the window that oversees what will be the Wingfields' house when they build it—they showed us the plans one visit, which seemed large, and imposing, and statusy and annoying, but what were we to do? Add our architectural advice? We asked if they could cut back a little on the height and they laughed. Why show us then? Everything is permitted, everything zoned. Our only respite is they're too busy to build it just yet. Right now, for this moment, it's an empty lot with shredded shrubs, and my father and my kid will lounge beside each other and enjoy some salty potato chips and watch the bunnies pop forth like it's a video game.

"Who do you relate to?" Dad asks her.

"What do you mean?" She is eight.

"There's the bunny. Who do you think you are in the scene? The fox, somewhere in the wood, watching? The circling hawk?" There was no circling hawk. "The bunny? Us?"

It disturbs her that "us" is an option; "Do I relate to myself?" she asks, scrunching her nose. They trade chip types. She likes BBQ. He salt and vinegar. "Too sweet." "Too sour." They're more alike than I knew.

My stepmother was a kind and productive woman, and I was grown when she came upon the scene so I didn't resent her; I was relieved he had someone to care for him, and when she got her cancer diagnosis I thought guiltily that she might not be the one, despite her younger age, to see him through to the end. I am an only, so if not her, me. She would've made a little bunny home somehow, I'm sure of it, would've dug them a warren to escape to with her bare hands. But it wouldn't have happened because she never would've lived here, had she lived. They would be together, up in Vermont, grilling corn.

My father says he used to be the fox and the falcon. He was, for a good few decades, all falcon. My daughter is still thinking.

"The bush," she says, at last.

"You pick a plant?"

"I want to grow everywhere," she says. "Make a home for all the things."

"Well, watch out," he says. "Somebody's cutting you up."

"I will grow back," she says. "Someday."

She's girly, and likes little pink dresses, is in one now, covered in chip bits. He's in his old pants with rubbed soft knees, his favorite umber wool cardigan.

"I will grow back," he says, wistfully.

In contrast to southern right whales, the North Atlantic right whale species has failed to maintain a positive trajectory towards recovery from the impacts of historic whaling. The reasons for this are complex but center on the far greater pressure from human activities in the northern versus southern hemispheres. The major known anthropogenic sources of lethal and sublethal North Atlantic right whale trauma are from collisions with vessels and fishing gear entanglement. These have increased in recent decades. Vessels have got larger and faster, increasing the lethality and frequency of collisions. Fishing gear strength has increased, with resultant increased morbidity and mortality from entanglement.

FROM

"Assessing North Atlantic Right Whale Health: Threats,
and Development of Tools Critical for Conservation
of the Species"

BY

Michael J. Moore, Teresa K. Rowles, Deborah A. Fauquier,
Jason D. Baker, Ingrid Biedron, et al.

PUBLISHED IN

Diseases of Aquatic Organisms 143 (February 2021): 205–26

For Pediddle

—

CHING-IN CHEN

1. They catalogued you #1012   [only 350
                                                                remaining]

a "right" whale easy target [hunted near extinction by 1800s
whalers]

first seen year of my own blizzard birth   [one human year may
equal

                                                                one whale year?]

you expected to live to 70 if not for –

                    "Not a single adult is known to have died of
                    natural causes in the last ten years"

                    your nine calves,
            two names - Contrail and Sickle –
and three uncatalogued calves in 1991, 1996, 2001 – who grew your
relations to four grand-calves and four great-calves

                    only one documented human-cause injury but a bright
circular leftside
            Headscar

                    Headlight searching for

daughter (Catalog #1308) killed by vessel

strike while caring for young
calf / Bay of Fundy > Roseway Basin > Great South
Channel > Roseway Basin > Bay of Fundy > Florida > Georgia >
Bay of Fundy > Gulf of St. Lawrence > Bay of Fundy > Great South
Channel > Florida > Georgia > Florida [yes with calf] [yes with calf] [yes
with calf] [yes with calf] [yes with calf] . . . . Gulf of

Maine [yes with calf] . . . . South Carolina . . . . . . Jeffrey's
Ledge . . . . . . North Carolina

>> North Carolina [no calf] memorable mark on upper jaw only
(propeller wound?) / memorable scar on mandible or lip / scar in

chin between left and right chin callosities / scar in front of
rostrum below bonnet / scar in, over, or touching callosity /

scar in or around blowholes / significant dorsal or

ventral peduncle scar (entanglement or other)

granddaughter Snow Cone entangled

5 times, first known

to have given birth while entangled, "almost
certainly

died" /
2020 calf catalog #5060 vessel hit
twice over at five or six months / deep rudder
wound

/ cut across tail ["When I read

the news

that Snow Cone's calf had died, I mean, I actually cried. It
was like

losing a friend, and now it's sort of hard to look at the
video from last year and the pictures of last year. It felt like losing a
friend." – biologist Sara Ellis] /

12 year-old great-
grandson Cottontail (Catalog #3920)
entanglement-dead– a line over head exiting

both sides of mouth extending beyond tail for 3–4

body lengths, 15

miles off Myrtle Beach, South Carolina coast who

grew ecosystem feast attracting seven

Great White sharks ["400 pounds of

dinner"], birds, fish, what's

left moving 1–2 miles

per hour

south

2. From mouths of Snow

Cone's entanglement

responders: "rope coming

out of mouth" "two trailing

lines from mouth" "tighten

over time" "through blubber,

through muscle, and even

into bone" "moving

24 hours 7 days a week"

seven teams recording

36 entanglements "keeping people

on bow as close as

possible so could throw

grappling hook

into her

entanglement" ["I cut it!

I cut it! I cut it!"]

"to cut rope . . . shorter" "if

    she can

then shed it

    on her own."
             "What

      I'm hoping

to see

    the next time

someone sees her

      is that there's no rope

         left

         at all."

3.
        As if some-

where in ocean, you

plankton-full frolick   migration slick   bump and splash   and rest   for long

    and rest   and rest   and rest

       as if gunshot calls   as if up-   through the miles

calls   as if scream and warble   as if progression we listen for

      as if searching   for family again   survivors

Bibliography

"2022–2023 North Atlantic Right Whale Mother and Calf Pairs." *New England Aquarium,* New England Aquarium, 1 June 2023. www.neaq.org/2022-2023-north-atlantic-right-whale-mother-and-calf-pairs/.

Fisheries, NOAA. "First Recording of North Pacific Right Whale Song." NOAA, www.fisheries.noaa.gov/feature-story/first-recording-north-pacific-right-whale-song. Accessed 1 Sept. 2023.

Helline, Meredith. "Body of Endangered Whale off S.C. Coast Attracts Host of Sharks, Other Wildlife." WMBF News, 5 March 2021. www.wmbfnews.com/2021/03/05/body-endangered-whale-off-sc-coast-attracts-host-sharks-other-wildlife/.

Pequeneza, Nadine et al., directors. *Saving the Right Whale.* WGBH Educational PBS, 2023.

The American pika (*Ochotona princeps*; hereafter, pika) is a temperature-sensitive habitat specialist known for its use of talus as a thermal refuge. The pika has been proposed as a sentinel species for climate change in alpine and montane regions, largely due to its exposure to the rapid changes in climate affecting montane habitats, as well as its potential for low adaptive capacity as a species with low dispersal ability and low fecundity, and its high sensitivity to temperature.

FROM

"Microclimate and Summer Surface Activity in the
American Pika *(Ochotona princeps)*"

BY

Lauren M. Benedict, Meghan Wiebe, Maxwell Plichta,
Heather Batts, Jessica Johnson, et al.

PUBLISHED IN

Western North American Naturalist 80, issue 3
(2020): 316–29

American Pika

—

SEAN HILL

Ochotona princeps

Like us, pikas spend their
days at the work of life. They wake
to graze and go about haying and try to
keep from being prey. Foxes, bobcats, coyotes,
eagles, hawks, weasels, so many get by eating
these rabbit kin with their big round teddy-bear ears.
And pikas prefer when it's no warmer than 78 degrees or
so to forage for grasses and make haystack caches for the winter
they'll stay awake through, and so they must contend with trying to
stay comfortable enough to work in this rising heat. Trying to find the
perfect spot to thermoregulate—stay comfortable—they tuck down
in the piles of rock at the base of cliffs, talus. The pikas' talus homes
sit in the rocky slopes of these Western mountains, which I also call
home, charmed as I am by their enchantment. My family's house is
a large precisely arranged pile of Victorian bricks built in 1893 that
has stayed cool, so far, these summers since. Some folks I love feel 76
degrees is the perfect temperature for living. At the edge of this town
are encampments of people trying to get by. Our pile of bricks has
been settling for this last century and a quarter and so is comfy for us,
its latest residents, thus far. How do unhoused folks settle, I mean,
feel settled? Like us all, the unhoused spend their days at the work of
life and trying to keep cool in this heat, like my family under our high
ceilings, like the pika seeking the cool deeper in the talus. I wonder if
we all can keep from losing our home, can keep from being the prey of
those folks who make hay in this latest and perhaps last season.

Novel approaches to jaguar conservation are needed because of the politics of the international border. New physical barriers and increased anti-immigration activity along this boundary (per U.S. Executive Order No. 13767, 2017) may further constrain natural dispersal to and from Mexico, isolating any potential jaguar population in the USA. In such a circumstance, species recovery would require establishment of a large population in the USA to ensure genetic viability and demographic sustainability. Conversely, if movements across the international boundary can be enhanced, an American population might be part of a regional metapopulation structure, contributing to long-term viability. In either case bi-national collaboration will be essential.

FROM

"A Systematic Review of Potential Habitat Suitability for the Jaguar *Panthera onca* in Central Arizona and New Mexico, USA"

BY

Eric W. Sanderson, Kim Fisher, Rob Peters, Jon P. Beckmann, Bryan Bird, et al.

PUBLISHED IN

Oryx 56, issue 1 (January 2022): 116–27

The Sublime Is a Foreign Species

—

SOFIA SAMATAR

Keywords: Ecological restoration, historical range, jaguar, *Panthera onca*, rewilding, spatial model, species distribution model, USA

Ecological Restoration

When he came along the riverbed, something came with him. He loped lightly, stopped to lick the ice in the crevice. Powerful haunches. Blue smoke breath. If he could find something to eat he would crush its skull. The wind whipped down the ravine with a dry, cold, tingling scent. Rock and juniper country, buff and maculate like his muscled coat. Was that what came along with him? Was he bringing the land its body? The golden, brindled lash in which it recognized itself. If he could find something to eat, he would begin with the heart.

Historical Range

Where is the jaguar? And how would we know? Photographs give some hints: this one, taken by Warner Glenn in Arizona in 1996, shows the huge cat crouched between stones, its gaze green with eyeshine, an effect of the tapetum lucidum, the mirrorlike glaze located behind the retina. Warner Glenn could not stop himself from exclaiming, "God Almighty, it's a jaguar!" A creature of shadow, rumor, myth. When Glenn took his photographs, the jaguar was still considered a foreign species in the United States, a wanderer from Central and South America. Officially, the jaguar was not here. It announced its presence only sporadically, and usually through its corpse, like the one an Arizona rancher exhibited on the hood of his truck before he was arrested for trying to sell the skin in 1988. We know the jaguar is here because we kill it here. Its hide is evidence, dappled with the distinctive rosettes, the black spots efflorescent with a pattern of lighter markings, unique to each animal, like a fingerprint. We know that in the nineteenth century, when jaguars were killed in Texas, Sam Houston sported a vest of such a hide. But we do not know where the jaguar is. In Virginia, where I live, Thomas Jefferson claimed to have seen a "spotted cat," but few believed him.

Jaguar

King of the animals. Largest felid in the Americas. Devourer of giants. Adorns the names of rulers: Scroll Jaguar, Bird Jaguar, Moon Jaguar. Hair short and bristly. Ears small, rounded, and black, with white or biscuit-colored central spots. Hunts at dawn and dusk. Belongs to darkness and the night sky, its pelt a star chart. Pale at the throat, on the belly, inside the limbs, and under the tail. Bringer of rain. Swims with head and spine above the water. Depicted with clouds, shells, aquatic plants, and sometimes scales like a fish. Pupil round, iris golden or reddish. Tongue flat at the tip and covered with sharpened papillae. Animal form of Tezcatlipoca, the Lord of the Smoking Mirror, manifesting at the close of a cosmic cycle. Fond of catnip. Represented with a vessel of water, a symbol of the moon. Skull robust, broad, and relatively short. Skull, excavated from the Templo Mayor, holds a jade ball in its mouth. When emerging from the water, shakes the body and each paw separately. Kills by ambush. Eats in a crouching position with its paws on the kill. Bears one to four young at a time, usually two. Vocalizes an atonal, pulsing, low-intensity cough or grunt, sometimes described as a hoarse bark or roar. Rakes the trees with its claws. Arouses thunder. Rarely attacks humans unless provoked. Most commonly found near water and plant cover, but tolerates a variety of habitats, including rain forest, savanna, marshland, and desert. Eats more than eighty-five prey species. Eats grass and avocados. Causes eclipses. When cooked and eaten, bestows the power to hypnotize enemies. Heart of the Mountain. God of the Underworld. Companion of shamans. Shelters in caves. Appears in murals as a plumed cat covered with feathers. Carries a blood scroll in its mouth. Will descend to earth in divine form at the end of days. Population decreasing. Born with its eyes closed.

Panthera onca

Panthera: Latin, from the Greek *panther*, probably derived from a Sanskrit word meaning "whitish-yellow." An ancient folk etymology links the Greek *pan* (all) with *ther* (beast) or *thera* (to hunt).

Onca: From the Portuguese *onça* (jaguar), most likely derived from the Greek word for lynx, though some say it comes from the Greek for hook or barb, a reference to the animal's claws.

Jaguar: From a Tupi-Guarani word denoting any carnivorous animal. In popular translations, *yaguara* means "the beast that kills with one bound." The related word *yaguaraeté* has been translated as "the real fierce beast," "dog-bodied," and "fierce dog."

Names: Limited. "There are moments in life when it is useless to call on reason," Alexander von Humboldt wrote of his encounter with a jaguar along the Apure River. Logic fractures. Normal responses break down. Experience expands so rapidly that language is left behind. Edmund Burke explains, "The passion caused by the great and sublime in nature, when those causes operate most powerfully, is Astonishment; and astonishment is that state of the soul, in which all its motions are suspended, with some degree of horror." For Immanuel Kant, the terrifying aspect of the sublime comes from a confrontation with the limits of human reason. A marvelous and obliterating shock. In chemistry, to sublime means to pass directly from a solid state to a vapor.

Unnamed: Sixteenth-century chroniclers report that people who lived near jaguars avoided saying the animal's name, a precaution they also took with the god of death.

Other names: *Tecuani,* "man-eater." *Zate,* "the one who eats life." A note in the *Codex Telleriano-Remensis* states that the earth itself should be called a jaguar.

Rewilding

A community in Asunción Lachixila in Oaxaca captured a jaguar that had been preying on their sheep. The elders recommended that it be turned over to Profepa, Mexico's environmental protection agency. The jaguar was transported to a reserve. But soon afterward, the people recalled that one of their ancestors had marked the boundaries of their territory riding on a jaguar, which was his *nahual* or animal double. They feared that without the jaguar, the land would decline. The local council asked Profepa to return the animal. It was flown in by helicopter, heavily sedated, and welcomed with incense, candles, and flowers. The people asked the jaguar to forgive them and invited it back to the nearby jungle, because, they said, it was their jaguar of light.

Spatial Model

Which spatial model are you using? The national model says the jaguar is not a U.S. citizen and should be stopped at the border. The highway system model says the jaguar may enter the country, but not travel north of Interstate 10, where speeding vehicles carve a line of death. The tentative conservation model adopted by the U.S. Fish and Wildlife Service says that local habitats can accommodate six adult jaguars. A bolder conservation model, proposed by a recent study, says that Arizona and New Mexico can support 90–151 jaguars. The climate change model says that populations at the edges of a species' normal range will become critical to its survival as the environment alters and conditions grow hotter. How do you think about space? Once, at a conference, I listened to the scholar Stacy Alaimo express her fear that humans can never care about creatures in the depths of the ocean, since we can only perceive them with the aid of complex and expensive technology, particularly the camera, an instrument linked to colonial invasion and control. Alaimo advocates a transcorporeal model, which says all bodies are fundamentally connected and interdependent. But it's hard to sense this over distance. It's hard to feel that everything touches everything when you're looking at a screen. Maybe a version of this problem applies to beings separated from us not by a vast depth of ocean, but by their status as threat: the ones we only see in photographs, or through the bars of a cage, or after they've been neutralized by a sedative or gun.

How to care for a source of fear, to see mythic terrors as vulnerable, to imagine offering shelter to what's beyond, excessive, outside? On my computer, I scroll through photographs of Macho B, the jaguar captured, collared, and euthanized in Arizona in 2009. The animal lies on the ground, one foreleg raised, caught in a snare. Is it only like this, with his swollen leg bulging on either side of the wire, his eyes glazed, his life soon to end, that he can command our sympathy? Macho B roamed a strip of southern Arizona for more than a decade. In an earlier photograph, taken with a trail camera, he is printed on violet darkness, his eye a drop of gold. I read that these cameras, used to photograph wildlife, are often vandalized by people who cross, like the jaguar, from farther south. They use the same pathway, the same model of space. It is May. White poppy thistle blooms in the canyon. A researcher follows the trail of a jaguar. But instead of a jaguar, he finds a man, alone and badly bruised from a fall. The man is screaming for help. His ankle is broken.

Is there a spatial model that would allow us to shelter what's outside without breaking it first? I watch a video of Warner Glenn describing the jaguar he photographed in 1996. At the time of this video, Glenn is eighty-one years old. Tall and rangy, wearing a white hat, he sits easily on a dry hillside. "When I looked at him," he recalls, "he looked like he had fire in his eyes." A little laugh of astonishment in his voice. I can scroll through pictures, but I can't feel the heat Glenn remembers, a flame that blazed through distance, consuming it. "He was locked onto me," says Glenn. His face is radiant.

Species Distribution Model

In the future, said the Olmecs, they will call us the Jaguar People, because of our artworks, in which the jaguar blends with the human figure. Look at this series of sculptures depicting a human, hairless and decorated with beads, in several stages of transformation into a feline. Look at this jaguar statue in the pose of a human boxer. Look at this human face with snarling jaguar teeth. Its brow has a furrow down the center like a jaguar skull. The jaguar is distributed in our bones.

Because we keep dogs, said the ranchers, they call us houndsmen. Because we keep cattle, they call us cowboys. These names denote our hybrid nature. We are distributed across the land at wide intervals, territorial as predatory cats. Listen to one of us, Warner Glenn, on the local news, describing his first encounter with a jaguar. He says our usual response in these cases is "shoot, shovel, and shut up": the jaguar, which might steal our calves, must die. But as for himself, he never considered shooting the creature. "Why would you? They are so doggone rare, and that's the first one I ever saw." He strokes his mule. He rides out with twenty-four dogs, listening for each of their distinct voices. When he photographed his second jaguar, he named it Border King.

Something is coming, the weaker creatures said. We hear it stalking. We smell its violent flesh. Its weapons glint. It is coming to destroy. Perhaps, among its own kind, it has quarrels and divisions, but we don't know that. We call it by a single name.

USA

The names. Patagonia, Santa Rita, White. The names laid over the land. The grit. The work. Getting up in the dark before dawn to tend the cows. Day in and day out, endless labor. Prayer. The ghosts. The wild. The joy of an indrawn breath. The elation of riding far away in the unmarked hills. The copper mines and the fear of the mines, the cash, the acquisitiveness. The protest. The well. The wall. The detention camp. The ruin of entire worlds. The immense loss and the remaining traces. The rags and shreds of life. The ones who eat life. The advanced technology. The innovation. The data. The roar of all those planes taking off at exactly the same time, the burning sky, the condo, the golf course, the mall, the highway, the military base. The spirit. The spirit of enterprise. The spirit of collaboration. The scrupulous care. The barn that stands for generations. The research paper by seventeen people. The tireless organization. The handshake. The bright and open gaze. The sentimentality. The almost unbelievable, cherished naivete. The unvarnished quality that makes even the elderly people seem young. Protean. Volatile. Never finished, even when so many things are lost. The willingness to start over. Bootstraps. The can-do spirit. The group project. The resentment of the group project. The longing for elsewhere, the mountains, the woods. The desire to go away. The desire to come back. To have something to show for it. The kill. The exhibitionism. The camera. The family album. The shock of distance abruptly perceived from the shoulder of a mountain. The rolling land. God Almighty. Its astounding elevation. The craving for the sublime: that overpowering, inhuman glare that leads you back to the hearth. But where is safety? And where is the outside? Cold morning light when the landscape glitters like a tapetum lucidum, Latin for "bright tapestry." The dewy plain reflective as an eye. Shadows of trees like veins. Far below, where the mist rises, there must be water. He licks his paw. He steps through bird and insect hum. Through glint and shade. This patterned, this perfumed. This blue and gold and gray. This blurring edge. This shelter. This now. This home.

Early-successional shrublands used by whip-poor-wills have significantly declined over the past century. In the Northeast, the proportion of forest in the seedling-sapling stage thought to be suitable for whip-poor-wills has declined to approximately 6% of the forested area, an average loss of 2.38% per year. These losses of early-successional vegetation, primarily resulting from increases in intensive agriculture or maturation of forests, have likely caused or exacerbated the population declines of other shrubland bird species besides whip-poor-wills.

FROM
"Breeding Habitat Associations of Eastern
Whip-Poor-Wills in Managed Forests"

BY
Kimberly J. Spiller and David I. King

PUBLISHED IN
The Journal of Wildlife Management 85,
issue 5 (July 2021): 1009–16

S

—

CLAIRE WAHMANHOLM

The story starts this way: a sea ago, there swam the smallest something. Then a spore. Then a seed sailed into the sand and surfaced as sprout, seedling, sapling. Soon, a spruce, a softwood stand; a forest whose synonym is *shelter,* whose synonym is *shield,* as in *shell,* as in *held,* as in *tells the self to hush,* as in *that which salves the sore. Sore,* from which *sorry* comes. And we are, standing among the sawtimber. We are, splitting it into shingles, subdividing the stubble, sending our satellites into space, from which we survey what's left. We are sore ashamed, slouching through scrub-oak, shrubland, sylvage that shelters the skunk, salamander, swift, swallow, snail, snake, stork, stag, sumac, squirrel, sparrow, spider, sunflower, saxifrage, sable, sugar maple. We are sour in our sadness. The sepal supports the soapwort's petals. The sycamore supports the sulfur shelf. We staked, stake, will stake our claims. The story is a soil in which we sow our syllables, which spread and spread, which speak of us as the only subject. We are slick as oil and sick from our spoils. We stand on the wooded shoulders we sliced a road between. We stick like sap to everything. We are sorry in all seasons, the snowy and the summer. Sorry for the silvicides in the silt and the surface water. For the spotted owl and the short-nosed seahorse. For the whip-poor-will's swoop and sally, its feathers secret and stippled. Whose song sounds like sequins, sounds like a stream, whose song shimmers. Sing, sang, sung, is that how the story will run? The whip-poor-will does not shelter its eggs. They survive through stealth, through something's sense to stay small as a salmon scale, small as a segment of a soft-bodied worm. The softest sphagnum step. We shelter in the study of the shepherd and steward. With science we scissor and scoop and sample, but it is a sweetless syrup, stoic and slow. We sift through scenarios. There is softness enough, and shelter enough; there is sufficient space and sedge and salt. But we are sore scared. Statistics shred the sinews that hold together a hopeful body. The nest is shrapneled. The holes in the sieve swell; things spill, spilled, will spill; the stepping stones are farther and farther apart, the shore farther and farther away. Sorry, I'm sorry, they're sorry, she and he are sorry, and we. Someone should surely save us. Should someday. Surely the story shouldn't end this way.

Snowy Owl *(Bubo scandiacus)*

ROOM TO MOVE

—

A snail living in a temperate forest may move only a few inches in a day. A tropical frog might never leave the plant where it hatched, living its life on a wide leaf and returning to the tiny amount of water held at its base to breed. Contrast their needs for room to move with those of a migrating bison, eel, monarch butterfly, or whooping crane. And then there are even more remarkable movers, like the godwit, a bird that flies for months at a time (8,400 miles or more based on recent research) from Alaska to Tasmania to warmer feeding and breeding grounds, or the humpback whale, whose habitat includes all of the world's oceans.

Animals move to meet their basic needs: to find air, food, water, shelter, and each other. Some move to have fun—or at least that's what it looks like to us: otters play in the snow, dolphins leap above the water, and crows chase each other when food is plentiful.

Some animals move together in groups and share their home ranges. These tend to be the prey animals. They include social herbivores like ungulates (even-toed cow-like and odd-toed horse-like), rabbits, rodents and their relatives, and many types of birds, insects, and fish. By moving together, it's easier to fend off predators and communicate to find food. Many of these species make long annual migrations by air, land, river, and sea.

Some animals are solitary, and most of these live in well-established territories. These tend to be the predators. They include members of the cat, dog, bear, raccoon, and weasel families along with birds of prey, large lizards like Komodo dragons, sharks, and some snakes. Most, but not all, are carnivores. (Giant pandas, for example, eat bamboo.) They are almost always on the move, to forage, breed, mark, patrol, and challenge competitors.

The omnivores are a mix; primates in particular can be social at times and predatory at others. Chickens, too. Insects are a whole other category. Most can fly as needed or at some stage in their life. Some animals cannot move at all except when they reproduce; sponges, for example. Others, such as jellyfish, require a current to carry them along.

—*Lucy Spelman*

Captive rearing of monarch butterflies *(Danaus plexippus)* is an extremely popular activity across North America, but recent scientific evidence calls into question the utility and ethics of captive rearing in this species. In late fall, monarch butterflies migrate up to 4000 km from the mid-western and north-eastern United States and south-eastern Canada to Mexico. Some studies have suggested that monarchs in eastern North America have experienced severe declines over the past two decades, with evidence, in part, suggesting that this may be linked to the widespread loss of their host plant milkweed. Each year, tens of thousands of educators, citizens, volunteers and conservationists engage in efforts to rear monarchs to adulthood (while minimizing risks), monitor their abundance and movements and educate the public about the biology and natural history of butterflies. However, recent studies have suggested that there is potential for long-term behavioural changes of captive-reared monarchs intended to be released in the wild during the fall migratory period.

FROM

"Captive-reared Migratory Monarch Butterflies Show Natural Orientation When Released in the Wild"

BY

Alana A. E. Wilcox, Amy E. M. Newman, Nigel E. Raine, Greg W. Mitchell, and D. Ryan Norris

PUBLISHED IN

Conservation Physiology 9, issue 1 (2021): 1–9

A Simulated Chance Is Not a Real Chance

—

ONI BUCHANAN

with quoted language from "Captive-reared Migratory Monarch Butterflies Show Natural Orientation When Released in the Wild," Alana A. E. Wilcox, Amy E. M. Newman, Nigel E. Raine, Greg W. Mitchell, and D. Ryan Norris, Conservation Physiology 9, *issue 1 (2021)*

Not sunlight passed through glass
not sunlight reflected off a mirror
not sunlight refracted through a prism
forced distribution of rainbows
not a shard of spectrum
not a filtered skylight not a mood lamp not a
head torch not icosahedral tangent slices of sun
to mitigate spherical distortion
not sun output of an algorithm
not a tearsoaked memory of morning or an even
beam passing through lace not erased
by blinds not hypothesized by night not
"ensured consistency of polarized light cues
supplemented by negligible foyer lighting"

> What we learn here is:
> a simulated chance
> is not a real chance

over a real amount of time
the time it takes to recalibrate
towards the real sun

It's true we grew up with no
active reference though as truly
any one of us—you or I—could say
"We were reared in captivity
with simulated environments"
"We drank synthetic nectar
an artificial source provided
ad libitum" "We first were flown
in the flight simulator
mistaking its dome enclosure
for the world Inheriting its terror
The vortex of inexorable blades
made 'stress-induced unidirectional
flight' our spiritual baseline"

The miracle is: deprived of all
knowledge of the sun we recognize
the signal once the actual beam
falls across the surface cells of our
antennae—The ancient mechanism
unlocks The compass needle spins

monarch butterflies do not show
normal southern orientation
even when exposed to sunlight
through a window during development
However, the possibility remains
that monarch butterflies released
in the wild are able to show

proper orientation if they can
calibrate their internal compass
with exposure to natural
skylight that provides external cues
critical to the functioning
of the molecular clock
that governs directional flight

        Turn towards the light Do you
        remember me?
        Do you remember this feeling?
        The right choice
        is covered in light
        That's how you know

Doesn't the tight scene control
strike you as lunacy disguised
as scientific rigor? Fattened up
by swamp milkweed *ad libitum*
until pupation then handfed daily
provided dishes with a 10%
honey-water solution within our
finely perforated mesh enclosures
humidity monitored hourly
using a handheld thermohygrometer
Plants watered twice daily
with reverse osmosis water
Soil fertilized weekly with
Plant-Prod Solutions fertilizer—?

        For you it all happens
        in the passive tense But there _is_
        choice here The violence

of arrogance *Your forgery of sun*
Your manicured malfeasance
Misdirection, sleight of hand

The environment "could be recreated"
or you could just give us the actual world
or you could just give us this one chance
this real honest-to-God chance
where the Given is that you're not God
The universe restored to "monitor our
abundance" No wonder I'm confused They fused
a flight tether to my thorax There's a reason
I did not fulfill at that time my natural
potential the big solve being for survival: fly
perpendicular to the false air current
before our panic sweeps us to the fan "The sun
fully visible through glass" "no surrounding buildings
could obstruct the view of individuals"

> Our exhausted brethren one
> by one deemed "temporarily
> compromised" showing "visible signs
> of lethargy" after being "tethered
> to a digital encoder" Each monarch "flown"
> entirely alone for just 12 minutes

Yes that space we could not name Yes that lapse
we could not connect By "acclimation" you mean
"reduce the right perception of the
fraudulence put forward" Annihilate our
instinctive nature Somewhere our cells
perceived the slippage We "could be flown"
or you could set aside your mediated sun

Technically your first conclusion
was true in the smallest sense, i.e. determined
without love without imagination Your
conclusive endpoint came too soon
Hemmed in by calibrations by
certifications *By fear If I filter it first If I've
cuffed the outcome to my assumptions*

> Yes we reliably failed again and again
> Millions of perfectly capable creatures
> prematurely "proven" to be deficient *What if
> beauty were given one minute
> to demonstrate a sign of
> flourishing Extrapolate it forward*

Our parentage is wild Unfiltered sunlight
the requisite to tap into our ancestral
code call it genetic predisposition God
awaken each animal in its mortal lifetime
Prepare us to receive Our deepest compass
turns us towards the sun Even you even
me We have an ancient birthright
of dignity We've made the passage to this
moment All the chiming unifies Witnessed by
adjacent telemetry towers our sentinels
of freedom We perceive at the conclusion
of our journey: the Butterfly Simurgh
is 41 "large individuals" outfitted
with a NanoTag and released together
in an open field in Guelph, Ontario

The recovery of Mexican wolves has been a tremendous endeavor undertaken by governments, scientists and conservation agencies in the United States and Mexico over the last 40 years. Today, more than 190 Mexican wolves roam free in two areas designated for their recovery, with at least 163 individuals in the United States and about 30 in Mexico. However, the long-term persistence of this sub-species will be enhanced with additional recovery areas, highlighting the need for a comprehensive analysis of habitat suitability for the Mexican wolf throughout its historical range to identify potential areas to conduct specific investigations of local conditions, both ecological and sociological, to select suitable release sites.

FROM

"Rangewide Habitat Suitability Analysis for the Mexican Wolf *(Canis lupus baileyi)* to Identify Recovery Areas in Its Historical Distribution"

BY

Enrique Martínez-Meyer, Alejandro González-Bernal, Julián A. Velasco, Tyson L. Swetnam, Zaira Y. González-Saucedo, et al.

PUBLISHED IN

Diversity and Distributions 27, issue 4 (April 2021): 642–54

Ahí Viene el Lobo

—

MÓNICA DE LA TORRE

The old approach captured
by "The only good wolf
is a dead wolf" adage. Now
captivity increases the odds
of its survival. Outlasted by forever
stamps commemorating legal
provisions—or rather, the lobo's
will to defy its endangered status.
Life span of six to eight years
in the wild. Numbers so low
its howling has to go further
in maintaining the pack.
I was wrong in thinking just
malignancies could be extirpated.
Fatalism will only take us so far:
as it turns out, they're still viable
in a territory larger than previously
calculated. The presumption
that their diet was unadaptable
to dwindling populations of prey
(ungulates, rabbits, small mammals)
led to erroneous assessment of the suitability
of various terrains. Causes for the shrinking
of their natural range include
cattle ranchers' proverbial hostility,
but not environmental destruction.
Add division between agencies north

and south of a border proved arbitrary
by the very continuity of habitats
for countless species on either side,
the Mexican gray wolf one among many.
Once the stuff of legend: *Lobo*
Lobo your name will survive
for no man could bring you in dead or alive!
Now its "majestic beauty"
graces correspondence no
doubt traveling more widely.

Hydroelectric power (HEP) is the largest renewable energy resource globally, accounting for an estimated 15.9 percent of generation in 2019. More than 8,600 HEP dams (>1 MW in capacity) are currently in operation worldwide, with a further 3,682 either under construction or planned. Dams may delay or prevent the immigration of juvenile eels, rendering upstream habitats inaccessible. For seaward-migrating adults, HEP facilities cause sublethal damage and direct mortality as well as migration delay or failure. Eels are particularly vulnerable at screens and turbines due to their elongated morphology and poor burst swimming capabilities.

FROM

"Important Questions to Progress Science and Sustainable Management of Anguillid Eels"

BY

David Righton, Adam Piper, Kim Aarestrup, Elsa Amilhat, Claude Belpaire, et al.

PUBLISHED IN

Fish and Fisheries 22, issue 4 (July 2021): 762–88

Senses

—

TONGO EISEN-MARTIN

Aquatic life now porcelain mythologies about fate one continent over
Where there is tide then life then gaps
Then pollutants then westward predecessors
Somewhere in this poem we are on a tv screen talking to sea citizenry
"You fight death, don't you?"
A quirky, twitchy eye death and distance from land
Close and personal power then settler colonialism
Death's step dad slapping audiences around
Less definable/More cage-able gods recruited by captains of the
 de-animated
"You spawn sentient, right?"
Behavioral drivel
 in the eye of the beholder
  before Columbus came

The historic distribution of Mojave desert tortoises was relatively continuous across the range, broken only by major topographic barriers, such as the Baker Sink and Death Valley, California, and the Spring Mountains, Nevada. Although desert tortoises generally do not move long distances over their lifetimes, historically, modest dispersal and connected home ranges occurred over a relatively continuous distribution across the tortoise's range. This contiguous distribution fostered historically high levels of gene flow and a population structure characterized as isolation-by-distance. Maintaining functionally connected landscapes is necessary to conserve historic genetic gradation. Large, connected landscapes also are necessary to facilitate natural range shifts in response to climate change.

FROM

"Connectivity of Mojave Desert Tortoise Populations:
Management Implications for Maintaining a
Viable Recovery Network"

BY

Roy C. Averill-Murray, Todd C. Esque, Linda J. Allison,
Scott Bassett, Sarah K. Carter, et al.

PUBLISHED BY

U.S. Geological Survey (Open-File Report 2021-1033)

Maintenance of a Functional Ecological Network

—

RAJIV MOHABIR

Yes, we crisscross the sky,
    the sea, the desert
with communications
    on how best to save
the earth, not accounting
    for the disruption
our intentions effect.
    Taking one tortoise
as example without
    land backing it:
water lattices, minerals—
    does not account
for the system necessary
    to bring up the sustained
healing of Mojave
    Desert Tortoise,
also known as gopher
    tortoise, populations. Habitat
conservation, road
    mortality, and landscape
disturbance, feature
    heavily, yes, but new
changes must crest with
    scientific discovery;

we must account
     for the fragmenting
of tortoise distribution, a diaspora
     caused by our hands, yes,
even us who require
     sustainable
and renewable energy
     are culpable for disturbing
the once continuous
     number, breaking them
into various groups with
     limited connectivity.
Scientists attempt to rewire
     the tortoise lines,
to interconnect
     habitat again
throughout the range
     of the species, providing
corridors through
     the desert, yes,
but also through us
     that we must maintain
even as we sit
     at our desks,
on our reading chairs,
     moving freely
across the world,
     requiring health
of not just ourselves
     but of any wild
life.

The Whooping Crane *(Grus americana)* is an endangered species with only one naturally formed remnant population which breeds in northern Canada and winters in coastal Texas, USA (Aransas Wood Buffalo Population, hereafter AWBP). Reintroduction efforts in a migratory population in the western United States (Gray's Lake Population) as well as the Florida Non-migratory Population were deemed unsuccessful due to improper imprinting and high adult mortality. In 2001, the Whooping Crane Eastern Partnership (hereafter, the Partnership) began reintroducing Whooping Cranes east of the Mississippi River to establish a population that summered in Wisconsin and wintered in Florida, USA. This prospective population was named the Eastern Migratory Population (EMP). Prior to reintroduction efforts, no Whooping Cranes remained in this part of their range although historic records occurred. Additionally, in 2011 state and federal agencies began reintroducing Whooping Cranes to establish another population of Whooping Cranes in Louisiana, known as the Louisiana Non-migratory Population (LNMP). It is important to understand dispersal patterns and population range expansion for ongoing reintroductions of Whooping Cranes to direct habitat conservation efforts and inform release strategies for captive-reared cranes.

FROM
"Natal Dispersal of Whooping Cranes in the
Reintroduced Eastern Migratory Population"

BY
Hillary L. Thompson, Andrew J. Caven,
Matthew A. Hayes, and Anne E. Lacy

PUBLISHED IN
Ecology and Evolution 11, issue 18
(September 2021): 12630–38

Poet Reads Science Paper
on Natal Dispersal

—

RENA PRIEST

Abstract

I'm guessing the study was funded
because common sense had to be proved
in order to convince people to stop
destroying habitat lest the species be lost.
I wonder if the people are moved.

Introduction

We're talking here about Whooping Cranes,
reintroducing them into the landscape and observing
them to *accordingly target habitat conservation.*
What if we gave the same consideration to people?
What if we were released from our cubicles,
and reintroduced into the landscape?
Would we *accordingly target habitat conservation?*
Would it be universal? Whole? Integrated? Beautiful?

Methods

Reintroduction Techniques

*. . . raised in captivity by either costumed caretakers
(costume reared) or adult Whooping Cranes (parent reared) . . .*

Though I wouldn't like to displace actual
Whooping Crane parents, I would like the job
of dressing up as a bird and raising chicks, please.
This is where science and poetry share common threads.
Both are sometimes absurd, but of the two, only poetry
is vital to the survival of humanity.

2001–2010 . . . taught to migrate south
behind an ultralight plane (ultralight-led) . . .

Ultralight lead me away! Unfortunately, poetry
is not funded like science. We don't get nine years
of funding to fly south in ultralight planes
with a flock of chicks behind us.
We're only called upon when people need
something said eloquently, for free.

Results

The study seems to have proved that
to preserve the species, we need to conserve
about six square miles of habitat in any direction.
pi*6^2, which is pi*36 ~ 113 square miles.
113 square miles = 72,320 acres.

Discussion

The information gathered in this study will help inform
managers of this endangered species.

It makes me sad that science seems
to believe that if the cranes are to survive,
some must first be captives, not free,

able to receive instructions
from their habitat and instincts,
not wild—managed.
What if science stopped playing daddy,
and god, and manager to things
it observes but does not love?
What if we tried loving the Whooping Cranes
and the places they live, the water they drink,
the glorious earth that sustains?
These are not questions that can be answered
with empirical evidence.
These are questions for the poets
and readers of poetry—for you.
What if you believed what needs no proof,
that it's all critically endangered, sacred,
and worth saving? (I'll bet then we'd see
more funding for poetry.)

American plains bison once numbered in the millions across North America. As abundant large grazers, bison played critical social and ecological roles in maintaining grassland ecosystems and cultures. In the 1800s, bison were nearly extirpated by European colonists for their meat and pelts, and as a deliberate strategy to displace and diminish native peoples. The establishment of protected herds enabled the eventual demographic recovery of plains bison. However, plains bison remain listed on the International Union for the Conservation of Nature (IUCN) Red List as 'Near Threatened,' and the ~20,000 wild bison that persist today are limited to several larger free-roaming herds, and many small fenced herds in Canada, the United States, and Mexico (each <400 animals).

FROM

"Challenges and Opportunities for Cross-jurisdictional Bison Conservation in North America"

BY

Liba Pejchar, Lissett Medrano, Rebecca M. Niemiec, Jennifer P. Barfield, Ana Davidson, and Cynthia Hartway

PUBLISHED IN

Biological Conservation 256 (April 2021): 1–6

The Bison Way of Making Things Right

—

JULIANA SPAHR

Right at the beginning of art: the bison.
There it is on the walls of various caves,
cavorting with the horses and the ibexes.
At moments, bison pauses mid-frolic, tail raised.
Sometimes bison is shockingly red.
Always beautiful. Always full of life, even when dying.
Is this not an art of what matters?
What comes after that is something else.
By which I mean all that art about the hunt that comes from the
    European eye.
Currier and Ives, Life on the Prairie: The Buffalo Hunt, 1862.
After Arthur Boyd Houghton, Buffalo Hunting: A Jamboree, 1871.
After Arthur Boyd Houghton, Buffalo Hunting: In Search of Buffalo
    and Coming to Grief, 1871
After Arthur Boyd Houghton, Buffalo Hunting–Camping Out, 1871.
Theodore Baur, The Buffalo Hunt, 1876.
Charles M. Russell, Buffalo Hunt, 1905.
Hunting the Buffalo from Fry & Sons Hunting Series, 1918.
And that is just what the Met owns.
They don't even have a cast of Frederic Remington's 1907 The Buffalo
    Horse,
the one that supposedly represents the unsettled west
but really represents a bison that was living in a zoo in the Bronx.

The reasons why there are thousands of representations
of buffalo hunts in state museums
and none of a bison on its back making the wallow
probably have to do with how Buffalo Bill Cody killed
over four thousand bison in eighteen months.
He shot sixty-eight in an eight hour period.
Always knew that guy was an asshole.
The railroad and the gun.
There is human ingenuity again, failing us.
And here is human ingenuity trying to pick up the pieces,
hundreds of years later.
Still, that Remington.
It is hard not to think there is art again, failing us.

When the bison wallows,
it is not just that the dust rises up.
They compact the soil, leave behind hair and oil from their hides.
Eventually this makes a deep impression
that fills with water when the rains come.
And an impossible art results,
the bison way of making things right
for the feathery leaves of the yarrow,
the purple or pink-tinted stalks of the field milk vetch,
the stalkless flowers of the cushion phlox,
and the wispy pink plumes of the prairie smoke.
Tall bluebells too, pendant bell-shaped,
next to the simple yellow flowers of the alpine arnica.
The bison way of making things right
for the woolly gray leaves of the fringed sage,
right too for the sage's small and unremarkable fruits.
Right for the roots of the Jerusalem artichokes,
the prairie turnip and the prairie parsley.
Right for the prairie chicken too.

The bison way of making things right for the male to come
hooting, dancing, tail up, neck sacks inflated all the while.
Right for the western chorus frogs
that come out at night to chorus and feed.
Right for the high jumping northern cricket frog.
Right for the small invertebrates and arthropods upon which they feed.
The sap-feeding herbivores with their beak mouthpart sucking on
    plant fluid.
The chewing herbivores with their mandibulate mouthparts.
And those that carnivorously feed on a variety of prey.
Right also for the grasshopper sparrow, also feeding,
and then creating a well-concealed open cup
on the ground
under the tall stalks of the big bluestem,
the shorter ones of the little bluestem,
the switchgrass and the Indiangrass too.

There was once a prairie.
It's never coming back
as in it will never be whole again.
There's the bison.
They can come back.
But the bison plus the prairie,
as in the bison moving over the prairie
with the rumored speed of a race horse,
that too is never coming back
until we change out hope
into something psychotic and large
in its demands,
by which I mean the end of capitalism.

Migrating birds can either minimize the number of stop-overs taken and travel almost non-stop to their breeding site (i.e. time-minimizers, such as adult male passerines in spring) or travel short distances, stopping and refu-eling when necessary (i.e. energy-minimizers, such as immature passerines in autumn). Such tactics, however, may not apply to species such as Snowy Owls *Bubo scandiacus,* which do not have a fixed breeding site that is their destination. After reaching the breeding range, Snowy Owls must prospect, apparently nomadically, as they seek out appropriate areas with high food abun-dance on which to settle. Hence, movements within the breeding range may be used primarily to prospect for lemming peaks, as Snowy Owls will only settle to breed in areas of high lemming abundance. In any year, these peaks are separated by large distances, so owls may assess lemming populations within the breeding range via stopovers to sample prey density interspersed by long-distance movements.

FROM

"Nomadic Breeders Snowy Owls *(Bubo scandiacus)*
Do Not Use Stopovers to Sample the Summer Environment"

BY

Andrea Brown, Rebecca A. McCabe, Jean-François
Therrien, Karen L. Wiebe, Scott Weidensaul, et al.

PUBLISHED IN

Ibis 163, issue 4 (October 2021): 1271–81

Flight Paths

—

JODIE NOEL VINSON

1

On a bluff above Minnesota's Root River, on land my parents purchased for retirement, stood a white pine with an eagles' nest woven among its branches. Almost every year there were fledglings in the nest and when you looked out the peaked windows of the A-frame cabin, you often saw white-crested birds circling the skies.

2

Eagles have a strong nest site fidelity, meaning they return to the same nest year after year, a behavior ornithologists call *philopatry,* "staying in the natal patch." An eagle's territory can be quite small, with other eagles nesting as close as a mile away.

3

A few years after my parents retire, my family gathers at their cabin on the bluff for the wedding of my younger sister—the last of three daughters to have "flown the nest," as my dad liked to say.

4

Other birds of prey—the snowy owl, for example—are nomadic breeders, winging over great distances to nest in locations invariably north of launch, but which otherwise move year to year, even by thousands of miles.

5

By the time our youngest sibling is married, my sisters and I live in far-flung places. I'd visited them in Belgrade and Boston, Minneapolis and

Myanmar, returning home to my latest city, which shifted every two to three years. For us, such kinetic living was an assumption, almost instinct.

6

This nomadic behavior occurs early. Out of a single nest on Victoria Island, one owlet flew to Hudson Bay, another showed up in southeast Ontario. A third made it to the far eastern Russian coast.

7

First flight: At sixteen, I tagged along on my dad's business trip to Florence. While he worked, I marveled at antiquity in the museums and in the cafés I drank dark, bitter espresso that made me feel adult. I spoke my first words into a cell phone, held to my ear by a young Italian so his friend could translate his proposition. I was charmed. Not by the young Italian, but by his city, by the scent of other lives. When I got back, I wrote a column for the school paper, urging my classmates to travel. The editor titled it: "Take a Pisa Advice."

8

Studying the migratory patterns of snowy owls, researchers discovered adults arrive to breeding grounds earlier than juveniles, incentivized, scientists speculate, by the ability to prospect and secure the best territory, usually one dense with lemmings, the owl's preferred prey. In other words: the early bird gets the worm. Another way of looking at it: mature birds are the better travelers.

9

In college I studied abroad in the Swiss Alps. My friends and I took to the rails, crossing borders without care, waving navy blue passports with pages emblazoned with eagles, wings spread in a symbol of our freedom, which in this case meant: to travel where we wished, to move about at will, to settle for a season in the foreign.

10

Migratory maps of snowy owl flight patterns, as traced by transmitters attached to the birds in backpack harnesses, show the owls tend to travel solo, sent by some silent call toward ice floes breaking upon arctic waters, taking to the skies without regard for national borders invisible to their otherwise all-seeing eyes.

11

The day of the wedding dawns clear, and my sister is married under broad blue skies. Listening to her vows, I recall the day my husband walked into the bookstore where I worked. We'd both grown up in Iowa, but left after college, arriving in Seattle within months of each other, where we'd landed jobs at different branches of the same bookstore. This parallel flight pattern seemed to extend into our futures, which, considering such shared territory, appeared, even in that first encounter, aligned—a forked river stretching below us toward some unknown bluff.

12

The snowy owl may migrate alone, but the birds follow similar flyways that trace the contours of the earth: valley, ridge, river, coast, and—in the spring—the retreating snowline.

13

The following day, a thunderstorm blows across the Minnesota plains. By the time it reaches my parents' cabin, winds have reached over sixty miles an hour. We stand on the porch as rain blows through the screens in sheets, whipping our cheeks pink until we flee to the basement and stare in daytime darkness at the trees slinging back and forth against a pale green sky lit with lightning.

14

Snowy owls hunt both day and night. Their eyes, almost the size of a human's, admit light on dark evenings, while, at the zenith of migration, twenty-four-hour sunlight illuminates the hunt.

15

The day after my own wedding, our plane lifted from Boston at sunrise, a honeymoon flight dripping in golden light. When I raised the shade for touchdown in Iceland, the sun was still rising, or rising again, our marriage blessed by the rosy rays of a contiguous dawn.

16

Later that evening, when the storm has passed, a few of us walk to the bluff to watch the sun set on clearing skies. As is our custom, we check on the eagles' nest at the edge of the property. But the pine holding the nest has been severed in the storm; the top half lies at an acute angle upon the upward slope.

17

When my parents first sold our house to retire to the cabin, I'd visited my grandparents' farm in Iowa, a cluster of three farmhouses, two barns, and a silo silhouetted against open fields, a tree line standing sentinel at its border. My uncle told my cousins and me the story of our German ancestor, who, a century before, dropped walnuts onto the spreading plains. I liked to imagine those pioneers arriving at what would be my homeland. This sort of rootedness appealed to me in my twenties, providing a backdrop to kick off from as I stretched my wings.

18

The average eagle's nest, or aerie, is four to five feet in diameter. Composed of branches woven into a conical shape, the nest is often lined with lichen and insulated with feathers. Construction continues over a lifetime—a pair may add up to two feet of new material each year, making it hard to say when this persistence is productive and when it becomes a liability, rendering the nest vulnerable to high winds that bend boughs until they break.

19

My flight from Iowa followed a different path than my grandparents and parents, propelled, like those westbound pioneers, by the prospect of a new horizon. On that first drive to Seattle, my car seemed to float along the flat Nebraskan highway as if it were a runway. As I felt myself about to lift off, I knew I'd chase that wide-open feeling of freedom forever. All my belongings fit in the trunk.

20

The nest of a snowy owl, by contrast, is a shallow depression in tundra, a hollow made by movements of a female's body against the earth.

21

Even in Seattle, I grew restless, and left the bookstore to travel. Back then, six months abroad felt like not only a rite of passage but an inalienable right in itself. *Do it now, while you're young,* my colleagues at the bookstore counseled, so wistful I didn't know whether to be sad for these aging adults with their untouchable wisdom or angry at the implication I might one day be grounded like them.

22

The aerie, which made the pine top-heavy as it swayed in the storm like a metronome, lies upside down—more beaver dam now than birds' nest, composed of sticks the diameter of my upper arm, wound and warped into a chalice. Even before we see the birds, the atmosphere has the thickness of a crime scene, that eerie ache of aftermath.

23

Somewhere along the way, movement became essential to self. Marriage didn't change that. One Christmas, my sister-in-law sends a throw pillow embossed with a map, across which, in olive green thread, she'd embroidered the flight patterns of our adult lives. I trace the stitches with my finger: Iowa–Seattle–Boston–Minneapolis–Seattle–Providence.

24

At the sight of the downed tree, I recall the row of poplars outside my childhood home in Iowa. When I was twelve, the stately trees sickened, and my father cut them down. Now, surveying the wreckage after the storm, I remember one of the poplars housed the hanging sack of a Baltimore oriole's nest. Staring at the ragged edge of the pine's abbreviated trunk, I see a flash of orange, a final flight.

25

When my husband and I decided to visit my older sister in India—even as the pandemic bled across the map—it was inconceivable our travels be halted by something beyond my control. Such privilege had never been curtailed or questioned; an autonomy ingrained into identity. Movement was my muse. Whenever I traveled, I liked to say, I came back with a story.

26

In the dimming light we spot them: two eaglets. We can tell they're young, not from their size, but because the birds show no sign of the snowy head that distinguishes the adults of the species. One eaglet, lying flat on the detritus, appears unconscious. The other is caught in a forked limb above our heads, wings like two great kites blown into branches.

27

Final flight: As our plane banked towards Boston on March 14, 2020, we didn't know it would be our last trip for some time. Just before we'd boarded in Delhi, I'd thrown up in the baggage-check queue. The airline employees were too busy escorting non-U.S. citizens out of line to care. I was ushered on board; those without eagle-embossed passports were grounded.

28

No conservationist returns our calls that evening, and as the light fades beyond the bluff I shiver at a distant coyote chorus. Then, late in the night, a call. Not from the DNR, as we hoped, but from an aunt. My grandmother had fallen in the night and broken her hip. It was hard not to imagine her prone in the darkening farmhouse, as she waited for help or, at least, for light.

29

Flying in to Logan airport, it can sometimes seem your pilot is aiming for the water. On several descents, as we coasted low over Boston Harbor, I'd checked the wings for pontoons, before the landing strip slid into view. Devoid of the human dwellings that densely pepper the coast, the airport on its flat, circular peninsula crisscrossed by runways, can appear from above like a desolate arctic plain.

30

As we stepped off the jetway and flagged our symptoms to the CDC, my mind began tracing our route back through India. I saw the drivers, hosts, and guides who'd ushered us through their homeland. I thought of the British colonizers of that country, in whose flyways we'd traveled, leaving disease and devastation in their wake.

31

Over the past three decades more than 300 snowy owls have been killed on North American airfields, with the highest incidence of strikes at Boston Logan. The owls are, with sad irony, drawn to this site of human migration: the airport teeming with terrestrial nomads, traveling in hoards because they lack the feathers to fly.

32

The following day, before leaving to visit my grandmother in Iowa, we check on the eagles. There's no sign of the parents, and one of the eaglets is missing. The other hops away as we approach. According to the raptor center we've reached, the fact that it doesn't fly is unlikely due to injury but because it has not yet learned to use its wings.

33

It's probable the airport's arctic appearance draws the owls, but we don't know for sure. "Nobody knows," Norman Smith, a man who has been catching and releasing the owls for decades, says in a 2018 interview. "We've caught about 800 snowy owls out there, and I've asked every single one of them and they've never responded."

34

Following our flight from India, we quarantined in our apartment, short of breath, flattened by fatigue. For the first time, I considered flight paths, who I might encounter, the impact of our meeting.

35

In the picture above his quote Smith is smiling beneath a moustache as he holds a snowy owl upright by its talons in a way that recalls nomadic hunters hoisting falcons into skies above Mongolian plains. The bird's wings cascade from what you might call her shoulders, curving toward each other so the serrated wingtips touch, as if she's clasped her hands, beak pursed in a knowing grin. But of course, owls don't have shoulders or hands, and when you look into this one's eyes all human proportions are lost in the depths of the dark pit swimming in mustard yellow.

36

As we drive toward the farm in Iowa my thoughts are with the eaglets— where were the parents? Would they return to their demolished home? It was hard not to put such sentiments on the pair of eagles that lost their nest, an aerie generations had been building since the sixties, a neighbor informed us as we pulled out of the drive—he can remember looking for the nest with his grandfather while fishing in the Root River as a child.

37

My freedom, I'd been taught, had been passed down to me at a cost; from the founding fathers to my ancestor farmers, sacrifices had been made to render me unrestricted passage across the earth. I was not told about the times when even such hard-won liberty must be sacrificed. That sometimes it's heroic to stay home.

38

At some point during lockdown, a former professor sent an epitaph from a gravestone she encountered on a cemetery walk: "Their strength is to sit still."

39

The milk-white feathers of the snowy owl camouflage its body against frozen tundra. To hunt in the unrelenting light of the midnight sun, however, an owl sits statuesque for hours before descending upon prey.

40

Inside my passport, unstamped since India, JFK declares: "Let every nation know . . . we shall pay any price, bear any burden, meet any hardship, support any friend, oppose any foe, in order to assure the survival and the success of liberty." What it doesn't specify: whose liberty? But another page calls freedom "the very birthright of humanity."

41

As we near my grandmother's house, my eyes latch onto that familiar silhouette of a tree line marking the borders of the farm that has been in the family for generations. I find myself taking the long view. I see a final flight. I wonder: Who roamed these prairies before my ancestors?

42

My passport also bears part of a Thanksgiving address from the Mohawk: "We send thanks to all the Animal life in the world. They have many things to teach us as people. We are glad they are still here and we hope it will always be so."

43

On Thanksgiving 2011, a snowy owl flew close to 3,000 miles to land at Honolulu International Airport, the first of its kind sighted in Hawai'i. Because it might interfere with air traffic, the bird was shot upon arrival. Imagine that final flight, those bleach-bright wings beating over unbroken blue.

44

Stories of snowy owls abound; the birds have engaged the human imagination from our earliest interactions. Cave paintings from 30,000 years ago portray two owls, identifiable by stunted bodies and downturned beaks, but otherwise rendered clumsily in rock, like a child's drawing, which feels accurate in terms of how close our knowledge comes to the species' cryptic existence across arctic plains.

45

Airborne between Seattle and Berlin, on a flight that might have been lost to memory, were it not for a photo: I'd just gotten a new camera, which is maybe why the picture has a clarity not always achieved through a plane window. Or maybe the light was right, angling low across the plains, it caught and pooled in every drift of the snow-covered landscape, these wind-driven undulations the only variation visible for miles. Across the center of the image, the curve of a dark riverbed cutting through Saskatchewan. An arctic terrarium, previously veiled in my imagination by maps that centered where I lived, stretched beneath me with such breathtaking vastness I no longer needed to arrive at my destination to know I'd traveled somewhere utterly alien.

46

In place of knowledge there's always myth, and when it comes to owls, we have plenty, from Minerva and Athena to Winnie the Pooh and Harry Potter. The owl, we say in our stories, is wise. Often, it carries messages. But true wisdom is in the storyteller who pauses, silent and still, to receive them.

47

Following my grandmother's surgery, we return to my parents' cabin. Circling the skies beneath the currents of a magnificent mature eagle, two fledglings take a first flight.

48

While each bird killed by a plane is a tragedy, the true existential threat lies not in an engine full of pearly down, but in the emissions that engine must produce to carry its human cargo across the sky, causing the planet to warm, reducing breeding grounds in the far north—the owls' room to move eclipsed by our insistence on mobility.

49

But in the years to come, the eagles do not return to the bluff. They are no longer a pet symbol for our happy home. As always, the story, the myth, the metaphor, is more complex than it appears.

50

I too have settled elsewhere, with an eye to live lightly on this earth, to leave but a slight impression in the tundra. The excitement of expanse is still with me. But I'm more resolved to stay grounded, to leave those bright arctic skies to you, yellow eye unblinking against the boundless day as you soar silent over Saskatchewan, snow-white wings spread.

Atlantic Sturgeon (*Acipenser oxyrinchus oxyrinchus*)

EACH OTHER

—

Animals live together for various reasons: to find food, water, or shelter; to play; for protection from predators; to migrate; and, to reproduce. The last is the ultimate goal. The most common social unit is a group of females with their young. The males are around but not necessarily in the group; they are busy marking their territories or competing for access to the females to ensure their genes are passed on. Less commonly, some animals live in male/female pairs, families, or multi-male/multi-female family groups. Some live in colonies, all male or all female; some can change sex, depending on temperature and other parameters.

For a type of organism to persist over generations of time, the individuals in a given population must reproduce successfully year after year, even when environmental conditions change. This is the definition of evolution, and variation at the level of the genome is required for it to happen. The result can be the appearance of a new species, the diversification of an existing one, or extinction.

Four processes drive evolution, and all involve reproduction.

The best known of the four is natural selection, made famous by Charles Darwin: favorable traits increase reproductive fitness in the face of changing conditions. The most successful individuals pass these features on to the next generation. Individuals with similar traits (e.g., the forelimbs of chimpanzees and humans, the pelvic limbs of whales and antelope) indicate those individuals share an ancestry. Until humans populated every corner of the Earth, the changes driving natural selection were, well, "natural." Now our actions drive so-called unnatural selection. Hawaiian birds, for example, did not evolve in the presence of cats.

The second process is less well known but obvious: reproductive isolation, or anything that makes breeding impossible. This can be a behavior, such as how a bird sings its breeding song, or a physical structure, such as a canyon carved out by a river. Human activity also creates reproductive barriers. Examples are many, such as a highway that separates a male panther from a female one, or dredging at the bottom of a river that blocks a female sturgeon from spawning.

These first two processes—natural selection and reproductive isolation—are nonrandom in that they are determined by the environment in which the organism lives. This is why our presence on Earth is so powerful.

The next two processes are random and seemingly out of our control. But not necessarily.

Genetic drift is the most confusing of these two, except for the fact that we all know inbreeding is bad. When an organism reproduces sexually, its offspring inherit some (but not all) of the genetic diversity possessed by its parents. In a small population, the rate at which traits can become fixed or vanish is fast. That rate is even greater when a small population is isolated because no new genetic material is being introduced. In a larger population, such trends are less noticeable. Genetic drift is problematic for an endangered species whose numbers are already low, and then we come along and make it worse. Introducing predatory peregrine falcons to the breeding territory of the red knot bird is one example of this; overharvesting oysters and leaving behind a limited gene pool is another.

Finally, genetic mutation is essential for evolution to occur. We hear this phrase and think, for good reason, horror movies. But the reality is we are all genetic mutants.

Chemicals and external forces such as natural solar or nuclear radiation can damage genetic material, but such changes are rare in germline (reproductive) cells. (Unless, of course, we humans cause a nuclear disaster.) Putting that cataclysmic thought aside, mutation is a normal part of the reproductive process. It happens during sexual reproduction as a result of minor copying errors which, thanks to the structure of DNA, are typically not a problem. The genetic material in the male and female germline cells is copied, divided, mixed, recombined, and divided again so each gamete has half the amount of DNA as the parent. No two eggs or sperm are exactly alike. When animals mate and the egg and sperm combine, the end result is a unique individual with a full complement of DNA.

Proximity is essential for evolution. No single animal will persist beyond a single generation. The result is a fascinating and amazing array of behaviors (and hormones and other physiologic changes) developed over generations that bring animals together at just the right moment, and an equally great variety of ways they ensure their offspring survive, ranging from fish that lay thousands of eggs at once to social animals such as great apes and humans that care for their young for years.

—*Lucy Spelman*

European ships introduced domestic cats to the Hawaiian Islands in the late 1700s, and within decades feral cats were noted in the wild. Today, cats are the only felid in the Hawaiian Islands, and unfortunately are common and widespread throughout the main Hawaiian Islands. Since their introduction in Hawai'i, cats have been documented to depredate a wide variety of bird species, including palila *(Loxioides bailleui)*, Hawaiian petrel *(Pterodroma sandwichensis)*, Hawai'i 'amakihi *(Chlorodrepanis virens)*, and Hawai'i 'elepaio *(Chasiempis sandwichensis)*, and likely impact many other species. In addition to cats' lethal predatory habits, they are the only known definitive host in Hawai'i of the parasite *T. gondii*, which causes the disease toxoplasmosis. *T. gondii* can infect any warm-blooded host, ranging from humans to both marine and terrestrial wildlife species.

FROM

"Quantifying the Presence of Feral Cat Colonies and
Toxoplasma gondii in Relation to Bird Conservation Areas
on O'ahu, Hawai'i"

BY
Christopher A. Lepczyk, Katherine H. Haman,
Grant C. Sizemore, and Chris Farmer

PUBLISHED IN
Conservation Science and Practice 2, issue 5 (May 2020)

Company We Keep

—

MARY-KIM ARNOLD

Does it matter where you begin
and when
the ships that brought
the men and animals
men
and animals

sickness gathering like wind
    cholera
    dysentery
    flu
    measles
    whooping cough
    smallpox

few natural defenses
the native population reduced by
90 percent over 50 years

*

Did a bird write this?
      I mean no offense
the scientists did their time
patrolling the island counting cats
all cats visible at any distance

cats present (y/n)
max # of cats (#)
supported by people (y/n)
feces collected (#)

the birds cannot defend themselves
few natural defenses

substantial impact on the population due to
    generalist predatory behavior
    and high mobility

*

The Gathering Place overrun by thousands every day
#aloha #alohaFriday #sunset #sunsetporn
#surf_is_up #paradise #discovertheworld
#islandhopping #influencer
#islandlife #islandlifeforever

People also ask
    Why are there so many cats in Oʻahu
    What do feral cats eat
Can I bring a stray cat home
Is it safe to pet a feral cat

(Support for this project provided by the American Bird Conservancy)

    What should I avoid in Oʻahu
    Is Oʻahu safe to visit
    Is Oʻahu safe at night

        Is there anywhere on Oʻahu that is not so safe

The Florida panther *(Puma concolor coryi)*, which once ranged throughout the southeastern United States, is now restricted to a small breeding population in southwest Florida south of the Caloosahatchee River. First listed as endangered in 1967 under the original Endangered Species Preservation Act of 1966 and subsequently receiving Federal protection under the passage of the Endangered Species Act of 1973, the Florida panther was and still remains one of the most critically imperiled large mammals in the world. Although males have been observed at various locations throughout the state, until recent years females apparently did not cross the Caloosahatchee River and no panther reproduction had been documented north of the river since 1973. In the mid-1990s the subspecies was near extinction with around 30 individuals remaining and severe genetic defects due to small population size.

FROM

"Location and Extent of Unoccupied Panther
(Puma concolor coryi) Habitat in Florida:
Opportunities for Recovery"

BY

Robert A. Frakes and Marilyn L. Knight

PUBLISHED IN

Global Ecology and Conservation 26 (April 2021)

Home Range

—

RAMONA AUSUBEL

We are moving into your house, which you do not occupy now because you are dead. Mothers should not die. You were the universe for me, and then you were a planet and now I am supposed to believe that you do not exist.

I can't talk about this with my children because I would be reminding them, or telling them for the first time, that I will die someday. Instead, I give them each a little plastic Florida panther figurine and a book about the beasts and tell them that we are moving to panther country. I show them pictures of the blonde beasts and their enormous paws, their white muzzle, black rimmed eyes. "There are only a hundred or two in the whole world," I say, and my daughter nods gravely. She had gotten binoculars for her last birthday. This, age seven, would be her best year yet. My son looks worried. "Panthers are not dangerous?" I tell him that they stay away from people, that they roam the jungle and freshwater swamps looking for rabbits and armadillo to eat. "Don't think of them as predators, think of them as magicians." He is nine, which is old enough to understand a lot about the rules of the world, and to feel discomfort with the vast unknown.

My daughter, upon the news, begins a study of the Florida panther. She says, "The species used to live all over the southwestern United States and now there is only one population in southwestern Florida. In the 1970s there were only twenty breeding pairs, but now there are around two hundred and thirty." She is seven years old and she seems forty. She taught herself to read at five with the fervor of someone who needed to know the survival manual.

"That's good," I say. "They're doing better."

She says, "They sometimes kill and eat small alligators and panthers are the leading cause of death for white-tailed deer in the region." She smiles wide at this because it means the cats are eating.

We are moving into your house because I can't get a job. The last academic interview I had was in a desert city and I flew in with my suit skirt and my pressed shirt. For two days I told person after person how prepared I was, how ready to teach their students to write essays. I didn't eat at meals because I was afraid of getting lettuce in my teeth and in the bathroom between talks and meetings I devoured granola bars and willed myself not to throw up. I tried to picture us there. To picture taking the wet, warm storm cloud of our family to that dry place. My husband was excited about it—he imagined desert wildflowers while I'm always simultaneously pulling away from and missing melaleuca, cypress, swamps. When the chair of the search committee called to say that they had chosen the other candidate I told her I understood but that I was now going to have to move into my dead mother's house. She was silent on the end of the line. That fury is still a flavor I can recall immediately. It's in my body somewhere, a stalactite in the cave, water beading off drop by drop, leaving the thinnest coat of mineral behind. Mineral that gathers and gathers and gathers until it becomes a dagger.

I'm telling you all these things because you are not alive to see them. When I had a mother I wanted no mothering, I wanted to drift in total randomness through space and time as if I arrived here on the back of a comet. I wanted to be a particle or an atom in vastness. Too bad I was landbound, feet attached to the dumb earth, body full of needs. I worked on a fishing boat in Santa Barbara, served biscuits and gravy in Corvallis, and in Santa Rosa I bent staves of oak into barrels in which wine might age. I stayed as far from Florida as I could, because you were there and I was the not-you. Even when I had a family, we kept our distance. Then you got sick and we moved closer. Now you're dead and we are moving to the very spot you left.

I sit on the small balcony of our Tampa apartment and drink a glass of water. It is hot and I have so much more packing ahead of me. The children have left their plastic panthers on the ground. I google the species. "Young males wander freely but females are reluctant to cross roads or the Caloosahatchee River, which makes them poor colonizers of new territory."

For six weeks—or, a space of time as long as the universe?—I have been surrounded by objects that feel like they are trying to devour me. I am engulfed by things you paid for, things you took in. Strays. Every pen, every sock, every piece of paper documenting a doctor's visit, an electric bill. Then I go home and am engulfed by our own menagerie: every piece of art created by one of my children at a gorgeous, singular moment in their lives. This gauntlet of art is one of the most excruciating parts of moving. How many must be recycled. Every time I think of their fat little hands, clutching a marker with intense focus, and here I am, eliminating that work from the world. Sending it to the mulcher. Motherhood is a train of monstrosity. We should be knighted for the things we are asked to kill. I am not in a ring with gold armor, a spear, and a lion. This is much harder: I am in a ring with my mother and a thousand versions of two tiny humans it is my job to love, and I must reduce the miracle down to something I can pack in a finite, practical number of cardboard boxes. The treasures are more dangerous than any wild beast: they eat their prey from the inside.

The boy is a minimalist. He wants puzzles solved, spaces clear, room only for books and important mementos. He keeps a marine protozoa, a white ghost of an ancient creature, suspended in acrylic. He keeps a toy Ferrari purchased in Italy. He keeps the knitted fox I made for him when he was tiny, little red pants, fishermen's sweater. Maybe this is saved because I am nostalgic, or maybe he cares about it too. Attachment is a habit we practice, our species. To love things makes little practical sense for survival. We are weighed down. We are bound to places that sink or burn or get twisted into the sky by swirls of wind. He will float freely, sail above us in an airship while the rest of us stand with arms full of metal and wood and plastic and jewels.

My daughter collects teeth. She has her own, each wrapped in a piece of tissue paper and gathered in a ceramic bowl. You'd never know what they were. Trash, or part of an art project, a candy bowl belonging to a witch. If ever she is in a rock shop she buys the tooth of a shark, and she scans the path for them, as if animals are always losing these pearls. It is only one of the things she collects. She throws away nothing she makes so her closet is an archive of cut construction paper, attempts to draw mice in the manner taught to her by a substitute art teacher, evidence of the phase where she drew pictures of her family as figures with only a head and legs. She has nubs of chalk too small to hold. She has been alive for only seven years, seven rotations of the earth, and the contents of that life is all here, the small apartment bedroom a museum of this tiny existence.

Last night, while I tucked her into bed in her nearly bare room, she said to me, "I learned that if you encounter a panther you should make eye contact but not run, which triggers their chase instinct. Panthers usually avoid a confrontation." I asked if it was like bears, where you put your jacket above your head to make yourself seem bigger. "The book didn't say. It just said not to ever turn your back."

"That's good to know, sweetheart. Thank you for the excellent research."

"It also said that panther kittens stay with their mom until they are two years old when they go off to hunt on their own. If I were a panther I would already be an adult."

"Let's stick together a little longer, okay? For me?"

I am sitting on a box in a living room I will not occupy much longer and I am holding the blue sweater of yours and I am asking for you, the ghost of you, who has not yet visited me, not in the wailing anguish or the bottomed-out sad or the bright peak of memory, to come now and advise about a pile of junk.

I am a cave of collected oddities, things gathered for someone I always thought I was running away from. I meant to leave you but all along I made choices based on your loves, your desires, your urgencies. Everywhere I went, you were an opposing force. What I didn't know is that you were not against me, that opposite my floating ship, you were my anchor; opposite my suspension bridge, you were the bearing. Now it is time to merge, my life in your home, the saw palmetto, wax myrtle, and Spanish bayonet you planted. Paths through sand, alligators that will outlast us both.

We have woken on this day, and the magnolia tree outside the apartment has flower buds that look ready to break with blossom. Or maybe I am the one who is ready. We are moving out of this apartment where our family has lived for two years. We say that word "lived" like it's a passive event, but what I mean is that we were sick here, feverish on the couch under a blanket; my husband and I had sex dozens of times in the bed that sits on the floor in the upstairs room; my daughter tucked stuffed animals in under a silk scarf she took from my sock drawer; my son stacked books on astrophysics under books on baking under novels about girls who can turn into dragons; we made and ate the meals that kept our bodies alive for some seven hundred days; we washed the same dishes in the same sink again and again. Is it reasonable for moving to prompt a sense of death? Or maybe it's this: you came here, to this Tampa apartment. You slept in it. You washed your face here, dried your skin on the towels we still have, now boxed for transport. I can picture you here. Your existence, in this way, is continuous. You will never have been in our new life, but we will inhabit yours. Will I become you? Will your ghost turn the taps on in the middle of the night to torment us? Will you fill our shoes with shredded paper? Or maybe you will be a benign ghost and leave gifts of flower petals, the coffee maker already filled.

On moving day, on the drive south, the children fight about the lyrics to a song on the radio. I turn the song off, which makes them angry at me instead, which was the point. I would rather be the direct recipient of fury than to live in a fog of bickering. "Tell me something you're excited for in the new house," I say.

"A bigger room," the boy says.

"Panthers, obviously," the girl adds. "There is plenty of suitable habitat in Florida for the panther. The challenge is getting the females to move into new territory."

"Moving is hard," my husband says. "Even for dads."

She counters, "Male panthers wander over large areas but females stay close to their mother's home range."

I squeeze my eyes tight and then open them wide. I do not want to cry right now. "Having a bigger house will be good for us," I say. My children are like goldfish that have been kept small by their bowl and now they need to grow, grow, grow. I have a second of panic that they will shoot upward so fast I won't be able to look them in the eye anymore.

My husband says, "I'm excited to never write a rent check ever again."

We pull up to the pinkish brown bungalow and I remember being a kid and seeing you out in the yard standing, just standing. It scared me because I did not know why you were so still. You were doing nothing useful, as far I could tell. Not trimming dead branches from the avocado tree, not weeding, not gathering the loose toys. Now I believe that you were hanging on to yourself like a person trying not to get blown off the top of a train. Responsibility must have been moving a hundred miles an hour beneath you. Dad had left. It was always me, needing tape to put up a picture of a horse torn from a calendar; me, needing to know if we were out of cinnamon; me, needing my hair brushed; me and me and me again. The house, too, was always hungry. New lightbulbs, a dripping shower, sticky spot on the kitchen floor, a front door that blew open, sprinkler head broken by winter snow. Your body was useful to us, the house and me, for so many things. I never wondered what you'd do with it otherwise.

We step out of the car, walk the concrete path to the front door, the four of us. The first time we will come here in this way. Home, even though it isn't yet. I take the keys from my husband who had them because he was driving. It has to be me that lets us in. It has to be me that crosses the threshold first. Are you watching us? I wonder. Are you hovering above, overjoyed, or jealous? If you were alive you would have a jar of lemonade sweating on the table and a gift in the children's room. Instead, the place will be empty. All sustenance and comfort ours to invent.

The door opens to the pale wood floors, a view of green, green, green yard through the sliders, which are open. And there, in the center of the room, lying on its side, is a cat. A big cat.

"Panther?" my daughter says. "Panther. Panther." Her voice is shaking.

"Okay," my husband says. My son is behind me, pulling me back out. The panther has a bird in her mouth. She looks at us but does not seem threatened. We all back away slowly.

Our eyes meet. Hers are a shade of yellow-black. She sees me, through me. Her body moves with breath and there is a low, nearly inaudible rumble. My voice knows it before I do. "Hi, Mom," I say out loud. The boy pulls me harder. The girl raises her binoculars to her eyes. My husband looks at me and then at the cat. He tugs my hand but I do not follow him back out the front door. The children do. I step forward and kneel down. I put my hands to my heart. "I like your bird." You curl your front paws. They are huge, and I can almost feel the weight of them draped over me.

"We're here to live in the house now," I say to the animal, to you. "You can stay around if you want. You are part of why we're here."

My husband beckons. "Honey, sweetie. Please come out." My son is crying. I remember that I am supposed to make eye contact and not back away.

Your muzzle is faintly bloody, I notice. There are feathers on the floor. You stretch and stand, drop your prey. My heart is beating so fast I can't hear anything else. This is the day I get eaten by an endangered predator.

This is the day I lose my mind. But the cat gives me a look, long and sure, and then turns, her long gorgeous tail sweeping across the floor, and she walks out through the back door.

I hear my daughter in my head, "Male panthers wander over large areas but females stay close to their mother's home range."

A big cat walks away through the grass, which is long from a week of late afternoon rain. A woman stands in her mother's empty house. A woman stands in her own house. The cat is a Florida panther. Or the panther is the woman's mother. The bird is a pile of blood and feathers. Or the bird is an offering. The woman is the mother. She is in her mother's home range. She is in her own home range. She is home.

The majority of Delaware Bay beaches rest on the shoreward edge of wide fringing tidal marshes. Since the last ice age, these beaches and marshes have been transgressing inland in response to a rising sea level. As the beaches transgress into marsh, mud and peat outcrops appear in and around beaches. Across the landscape, this process results in a mosaic of sandy beaches with varying depths of sand interspersed with peat and residual salt marsh at the foot of beach slopes. American horseshoe crabs appear to avoid areas of mud and peat, and high-quality habitat is characterized by continuous deep sand that offers adequate oxygen levels and minimizes exposure of developing eggs to hydrogen sulfide. Given this pattern, horseshoe crab habitat availability is influenced by beach transgression, with temporal and spatial variation in habitat quality depending on both long-term (e.g. sea level rise) and short-term (e.g. storms) disturbances.

FROM

"Beach Restoration Improves Habitat Quality for American Horseshoe Crabs and Shorebirds in the Delaware Bay, USA"

BY

Joseph A. M. Smith, Lawrence J. Niles, Steven Hafner, Aleksandr Modjeski, and Tim Dillingham

PUBLISHED IN

Marine Ecology Progress Series 645 (July 2020): 91–107

Blood Price

—

DONIKA KELLY

I've done my best not to think
of horseshoe crabs
their blue blood
their decade spent unsurveilled
the three hundred million years
they have passed subject
to the comet's the shark's
the gull's descending eye

Without thinking I mirror
how little they must think of us
How unimaginable we must be

Our unimaginable industry
gathering the material meant
to recover what ought
to have remained buried
while the beach transgresses
into the marsh and the marsh
transgresses into the interior
the beach
a memory
the peat and hard structures
revealed after storm and surge
all that remains

Our industry is approximate
the sand to our eye fine
the sand to the horseshoe crabs' legs
too fine to dig a hole to set the egg cluster
that feeds the terrapin and red knot
and ruddy turnstone

I want to think of the crab now
a boon but distant companion
but we devastate with our virtue
late and meager
    still I say we
because how dare I distinguish
one animal from the other

Atlantic Sturgeon (*Acipenser oxyrinchus*) are endangered throughout much of their U.S. range as a result of multiple threats where the associated risks are dependent on life history phase. The Hudson River is estimated to support the largest population of Atlantic Sturgeon in the United States, with an estimate of less than 1,000 spawning adults. Despite being the largest population, the Hudson River Atlantic Sturgeon are listed as endangered under the New York Bight distinct population segment and continually face threats such as disturbances from the shipping industry, energy development, and poaching when occupying the river. Despite a full moratorium on harvest in 1996 and the endangered listing, there is still a continued need for efforts to support conservation and recovery.

FROM

"Spawning Intervals, Timing, and Riverine Habitat Use
of Adult Atlantic Sturgeon in the Hudson River"

BY

M. W. Breece, A. L. Higgs, and D. A. Fox

PUBLISHED IN

Transactions of the American Fisheries Society 150,
issue 4 (July 2021): 528–37

Ancient Music

—

KYOKO MORI

Of all the animals who share our planet, fish are the hardest to know and love as companions. The wild species spend their lives underwater, their daily habits, seasonal migrations, and life cycles hidden from us. The tropical fish in our home aquariums seem more ornamental than companionable: the glitter of neon tetras, the swirl of angelfish, the fragile delicacy of glass catfish—so pretty in a desultory, distant way. Except for the fleeting seconds they rise to the surface to interact, more with the food we sprinkle than with us, they are hardly distinguishable from the pebbles, artificial seaweed, and plastic castles that decorate their make-believe world under the sea. Although most fish in aquariums are bred in captivity, they are fundamentally different from the cats, dogs, rabbits, hamsters, parakeets, geckos, or even hermit crabs and tarantulas we keep as pets. We cannot touch them. We do not breathe the same element. What gives us life will kill them after a short exposure. What sustains them will drown the best swimmers among us after a few hours at sea without intervention or stop our hearts immediately with hypothermia.

When people give up eating meat, they usually start by omitting mammals—cows, pigs—from their diet and soon after, chickens and turkeys. Fish are the last to come off the plate. This may be because, all our lives, we've been told the benefits of fish consumption (low in cholesterol, "brain food," etc.). But it's also because for most humans, turning cows and pigs into food is uncomfortably close to devouring our dogs and cats. The situation is further complicated by a few mammals, such as rabbits and horses, that are eaten by some and cared for by others. Tucking into a filet of salmon or a whole trout arrayed on a platter does not cause the same level of discomfort for most diners. My own journey to becoming a vegetarian was different because I grew up in Japan, where any four-year-old accompanying her mother to the market would find herself eye-level with a slab of ice on a wooden platform and, spread across its slick expanse, a dozen fish laid out in profile, their dead eyes wide open. I didn't give up eating fish; I never started. Although I always balked at the idea of eating anything that had to be killed, I was 26 before I stopped consuming any fellow creature on our planet, not even to be polite to the chef. The Atlantic sturgeon, whose migration into the Hudson River was the subject of a scientific study between 2010 and 2016, is currently listed as an endangered species due to habitat loss and to centuries of overfishing for its eggs, a source of caviar. A "living fossil" that has existed for some 250 million years, the sturgeon, whose body is armored with five rows of bony plates known as scutes, indeed looks prehistoric. It has a long snout, five barbels like a scraggly beard under the chin, and a lopsided tail. Some individuals can live 60 years and grow to be 14 feet long and weigh 800 pounds. Although most sturgeon in the South Atlantic are thought to live only (!) 25 to 30 years, they do not reach their maturity until they are about 11 years old. The 391 caught off the coast of Delaware for the Hudson River study were between 40 cm and 236 cm (7.74 feet), and only those longer than 130 cm, likely to be full-grown adults ready to spawn, were tagged for tracking. If you watch the YouTube videos of the capture and the tagging, the fish held in a net on the side of the boat will remind you of certain breeds of retrievers: aerodynamic, spotted, temporarily calm. The whole species will strike you, suddenly, as not so alien.

Sturgeon are anadromous: born in freshwater, they spend most of their adulthood in the coastal waters of the ocean except when they return to their natal river to spawn. Unlike the shorter-living salmon—most (though not all) of which only spawn once and die—the sturgeon can spawn multiple times over their decades-long life cycle. The majority of the tagged sturgeon that returned to the Hudson did so every year, every other year, or every third year. The species' population has not recovered in spite of this seeming productivity and the fishing moratorium that has been in place since 1994. Their mortality continues to be high due to environmental degradation and human structures and activities such as dams, boat traffic, gillnet fishing (for other fish), and dredging. The study confirmed that the adult sturgeon were present in the Hudson between May and July and recommended that human activities should be curtailed during those months; it also identified the specific segments of the river where the females laid their eggs so the young fish that hatched from them could be protected until they, too, swim downstream and exit the river in September.

Fish migrate through rivers and oceans for the same reasons that birds traverse the sky over continents: to grow into adulthood where the food is abundant and to reproduce where their offspring have the best chance of survival. Even without binoculars, we can see birds in the sky, on the ground in our yard, or in the trees at a city park. Thanks to popular nature shows and movies, most of us are aware of bird migration and familiar with the work of bird-banding volunteers and scientists who monitor the population fluctuations and the health of various songbird species. Tracking sturgeon with telemetry tags is similar and different. Small songbirds can be tracked only if a banded bird either falls to the ground and is recovered, or if it flies into the mist net at another banding site or in another year. Telemetry tags for fish are more like the radar tags used in tracking larger birds (such as birds of prey) or mammals on the ground: the individual doesn't have to be caught again to be tracked.

The tagged sturgeon made a "ping" every time they swam past the 63 acoustic stations along the Hudson River from the Verrazzano-Narrows Bridge at its mouth to the town of Schodack, 215 miles upstate. The graphs drawn to indicate the pattern of the recorded "pings"—the box plots of arrival and departure dates for the sturgeon—resemble musical notations, not the five-line staves of modern-day musical score but the simpler marks that preceded them, used in the Middle Ages for Gregorian chants. As the male, female, and unidentified (those that could not be sexed when caught initially) sturgeon swam past the acoustic receivers, each group struck a slightly different note. I'm not sure what the underwater pings sounded like, but I can imagine the sturgeon swimming up the river in spring and returning to the sea in midsummer, each leg of the journey a three-part harmony. The music of the sturgeon migration, even if we cannot hear it, should make us understand that fish are not alien to us. Their inability to speak or sing, purr in contentment, bark in warning, or yelp and screech in distress has no doubt contributed to our perception of fish as guilt-free sources of food ("they don't even have a brain or a nervous system," people often say). Now we can listen for their movement through the most iconic city of our nation.

A small segment of the study area is on my migration route. Although I've never lived in New York, it's a city I visit regularly, and the path over and along the Hudson River between the Upper West Side and the West 30s is where I run: south through Riverside Park from 108th Street to the Dog Run, down the footpath on 72nd Street to the waterfront, along the running/cycling path to the Hudson Yards. It's a point-to-point route, downstream first, turning around at the Javits Center and heading back upstream. On every run, I'm aware of the strata of sound that surround me: the planes in the sky, the birds in the trees, the cars on the road, construction and delivery vehicles on the docks, the runners and cyclists on the path, and the water flowing down the river and sloshing against the embankment. I haven't returned to the Hudson since encountering the study, but if my next run happens between May and July, I'll listen for the base notes of the sturgeon in the river below. A strain of ancient music, their migration anchors the world we move through, breathing air, water, air, water.

The eastern population of peregrine falcons *(Falco peregrinus)* experienced a precipitous decline throughout the 1950s, was believed to have been extirpated by the early 1960s and was listed as federally 'endangered' in June 1970. In 1975, the U.S. Fish and Wildlife Service appointed an Eastern Peregrine Falcon Recovery Team to develop and implement a Recovery Plan. As part of this plan, the team released 307 captive-reared falcons (1975–1985) on artificial structures within the mid-Atlantic Coastal Plain, a physiographic region with no historic breeding population. The decision was based on the fact that both prey availability and fledgling return rates were higher on the Coastal Plain compared to the historic mountain range. The effort followed a single-species set of objectives with no consideration of the broader community. By 2007 the population had reached 55 breeding pairs (all nesting on artificial substrates) and was self-sustaining. Pairs on the outer coast have adjusted their breeding phenology to match the period of highest metabolic demand to the peak passage of shorebirds. Diet during the brood-rearing period is dominated by migrating shorebirds including red knots.

FROM
"Influence of Introduced Peregrine Falcons on the Distribution of Red Knots within a Spring Staging Site"

BY
Bryan D. Watts and Barry R. Truitt

PUBLISHED IN
PLoS ONE 16 (January 2021): 1–12

proximal influence

—

ASIYA WADUD

for every knot who relays the logic of the Arctic
it begins in credence
gesticulating its daylong burden
          billows for the ever-reaching

               throughway, habitual in its widening arc
               whereas decadence or logic meets decay

with our own human intuition, a study handed to each
          of us in boundary
the frontier widens, the frontier lifts,
eyries contained, domesticated

               a proxy for every pair of hands that lifts
                    passage or peripheral logic

a whole gilded world holds the peregrine
     kingdom rests on its disciplined range
     kingdom rests on its myopic vision
kingdom holds all its want
its appetite unfinished

                         the singular logic of the question, weighted
                              singularity narrows the credence

          every world   a consummation of I
     slinking in its logic so I
     tunneled through the habitat and I

its reverence made opulent in credence
belief becomes threefold
    no matter the red knots'
           need

the peregrine is a world, doubled and felled
reigning over its diminished scope
a haven for each yearning

         a proxy for every pair of hands that lifts
         the edge and stretches it—
            pared to the thrill
         filament in the act of reaching

The Olympia oyster *(Ostrea lurida)* is the only oyster species native to the west coast of North America north of Baja California Sur, Mexico, where it creates habitat for numerous estuarine and coastal species, and supported a once vital fishery dating back to pre-colonial history. Populations have declined precipitously due to human-induced impacts including overharvest, the alteration of estuarine habitats, poor water quality, sedimentation, introduced predators, and a changing climate. As a result, Olympia oyster populations are estimated to be at 1% of historic levels and face local extinction in some regions.

FROM

"Conservation of Marine Foundation Species:
Learning from Native Oyster Restoration
from California to British Columbia"

BY

April D. Ridlon, Althea Marks, Chela J. Zabin,
Danielle Zacherl, Brian Allen, et al.

PUBLISHED IN

Estuaries and Coasts 44 (2021): 1723–43

Restoration Challenges

—

JANE WONG

When I first shucked an oyster, I nearly
                    fell over, the hinge opening when I least
expected it, like my absent father calling
                    ten years later asking in Toisanese *how are*
you where are you now as if nothing had
                    happened, as if the shell had always been
ajar, bacteria floating through like chimney
                    smoke. I held the knife in my hand, salt
startled, a letter opener to what speckled
                    message? These days, I am thinking about
restoration. How to restore the heart, that
                    tidal current. How the land is in need of
restoration, always, because we do what
                    we do to it. I read about how raccoons
were observed preying on native oysters,
                    imagine their paws pearling the mud flats
clean. Briny organ slipping down their
                    throats, furred hunger. Or maybe it's
the sea star, wrapping its arms around
                    the bivalve, clinging to something, anything –
I don't blame them. I, too, want to press
                    reset. As in: *oh I'm good, I live in the Pacific*
Northwest. To think it's that easy. Somewhere,
                    history is shaking its buried head. What heals,
here, will take time and time and—

Contributors

Kazim Ali is the author of *Northern Light: Power, Land, and the Memory of Water* and seven collections of poetry *(Sunken: New and Selected Poems; The Voice of Sheila Chandra; Inquisition; All One's Blue; Sky Ward*, winner of the Ohioana Book Award in Poetry; *The Fortieth Day*; and *The Far Mosque)*, as well as the cross-genre texts *Bright Felon* and *Wind Instrument*.

Mary-Kim Arnold is a writer, artist, and administrator of higher education, currently serving as Dean of the Faculty and Academic Affairs at Vermont College of Fine Arts. She is the author of *The Fish & the Dove: Poems* and *Litany for the Long Moment*. A transnational, transracial Korean-born adoptee, her text and textile work explore themes of hybridity, dislocation, racial and cultural identity, and gender. She is senior editor for collaborative and cross-disciplinary texts at *Tupelo Quarterly*.

Ramona Ausubel is the author of three novels and two story collections, among them *The Last Animal, Awayland,* and *Sons and Daughters of Ease and Plenty.* She has received the PEN Center USA Literary Award for Fiction and the VCU Cabell First Novelist Award and has been longlisted for the Story Prize. Her writing has been published in *The New Yorker, The New York Times,* and NPR's Selected Shorts. She is a professor at Colorado State University.

David Baker is the author or editor of nineteen books, including thirteen books of poetry, most recently *Whale Fall, Swift: New and Selected Poems, Scavenger Loop,* and *Never-Ending Birds,* which was awarded the Theodore Roethke Memorial Poetry Prize, and six books of prose, including *Seek After: On Seven Modern Lyric Poets.* His poems and essays have been published in *American Poetry Review, The Atlantic Monthly, The Nation, The New Criterion, The New Republic, The New York Times, The New Yorker, The Paris Review, Poetry, Raritan, Tin House,* and *The*

Yale Review. He was poetry editor of *The Kenyon Review* for more than twenty-five years and currently curates the annual "Nature's Nature" feature for the magazine. He is a teaching emeritus professor of English at Denison University.

Charles Baxter is author of the novels *The Feast of Love* (nominated for the National Book Award), *First Light, Saul and Patsy, Shadow Play, The Soul Thief,* and *The Sun Collective,* and the story collections *Believers, Gryphon, Harmony of the World, A Relative Stranger, There's Something I Want You to Do,* and *Through the Safety Net.* His stories have been published in several anthologies, including *The Best American Short Stories, The Pushcart Prize Anthology,* and *The O. Henry Prize Story Anthology.* He has won the PEN/Malamud Award for Excellence in the Short Story.

Aimee Bender is the author of six books of fiction, including *The Girl in the Flammable Skirt,* a *New York Times* Notable Book; *The Particular Sadness of Lemon Cake,* which won the SCIBA award; and *The Butterfly Lampshade,* longlisted for the PEN/Jean Stein Award. Her books have been translated into sixteen languages, and her short fiction has been published in *Granta, Harper's, Tin House, McSweeney's,* and *The Paris Review.*

Kimberly Blaeser, past Wisconsin Poet Laureate and founding director of Indigenous Nations Poets, is the author of six poetry collections, most recently *Ancient Light, Copper Yearning,* and the bilingual *Résister en dansant/Ikwe-niimi: Dancing Resistance.* She edited *Traces in Blood, Bone, and Stone: Contemporary Ojibwe Poetry* and wrote the monograph *Gerald Vizenor: Writing in the Oral Tradition.* Her photographs and picto-poems have been featured in exhibits such as *No More Stolen Sisters.* An enrolled member of the White Earth Nation, she is an Anishinaabe activist and environmentalist whose accolades include a Lifetime Achievement Award from Native Writers' Circle of the Americas. She is the 2024 Mackey Chair in Creative Writing at Beloit College, an MFA faculty member at the Institute of American Indian Arts, and a professor emerita at University of Wisconsin–Milwaukee.

Oni Buchanan has written four poetry books: *Time Being, Must a Violence, Spring,* and *What Animal.* She is the cofounder and CEO of ImmerSphere, an augmented reality content creation and publishing platform for storytellers of the future. She is also the founder and director of Ariel Artists, a music management company representing innovative performers with a driving passion for artistic exploration and interdisciplinary inquiry.

Tina Cane is the founder and director of Writers-in-the-Schools, RI, and served as poet laureate of Rhode Island from 2016 to 2024. She is the author of *The Fifth Thought, Dear Elena: Letters for Elena Ferrante* (poems with art by Esther Solondz), *Once More with Feeling, Body of Work,* and *Year of the Murder Hornet.* She has received the Fellowship Merit Award in Poetry from the Rhode Island State Council on the Arts and was a 2020 Poet Laureate Fellow with the Academy of American Poets. *Alma Presses Play,* her novel-in-verse for young adults, was published in 2021. Her second novel-in-verse for young readers, *Are You Nobody, Too?,* was released in the summer of 2024. She is the creator and curator of the distance-reading series Poetry Is Bread and editor of the forthcoming *Poetry Is Bread: The Anthology.*

Descended from ocean dwellers, **Ching-In Chen** is a genderqueer Chinese American writer, community organizer, and teacher. They are author of *The Heart's Traffic: a novel in poems* and *recombinant* (which received the 2018 Lambda Literary Award for Transgender Poetry), as well as the chapbooks *to make black paper sing* and *Kundiman for Kin :: Information Retrieval for Monsters.* Chen is coeditor of *The Revolution Starts at Home: Confronting Intimate Violence within Activist Communities,* a Massage Parlor Outreach Project core member, and a Kelsey Street Press collective member. They received fellowships from Kundiman, Lambda, Can Serrat, Imagining America, the Jack Straw Cultural Center, and the Intercultural

Leadership Institute as well as the Judith A. Markowitz Award for Exceptional New LGBTQ Writers. They are working on *Breathing in a Time of Disaster,* a performance, installation, and speculative writing project exploring breath through meditation, health, and environmental justice. They teach at University of Washington Bothell. www.chinginchen.com.

Mónica de la Torre is a poet and scholar. Her full-length poetry collections include *Pause the Document, Repetition Nineteen, The Happy End / All Welcome,* and *Public Domain.* She teaches at Brooklyn College.

Originally from San Francisco, **Tongo Eisen-Martin** is a poet, movement worker, and educator. His curriculum on extrajudicial killing of Black people, *We Charge Genocide Again,* has been an educational and organizing tool throughout the country. He is the author of *Someone's Dead Already, Heaven Is All Goodbyes, Waiting Behind Tornados for Food,* and *Blood on the Fog.* He cofounded Black Freighter Press to publish revolutionary works and is San Francisco's eighth poet laureate.

Thalia Field has published several collections of experimental texts with New Directions, most recently *Personhood* and *Bird Lovers, Backyard.* Her novel *Experimental Animals (A Reality Fiction)* is about the origins of the scientific laboratory and the animal rights movement in the nineteenth century. Thalia has collaborated with French author Abigail Lang on *Leave to Remain (Legends of Janus)* and *A Prank of Georges,* and Thalia's most recent collaborations with sound designer and artist Ben Williams are available at www.category-other.com. Thalia teaches in the literary arts department at Brown University and is most proud to work whenever possible as an animal rehabber under the guidance of the incredible Sheida Soleimani and Arianna Mouradjian.

Ben Goldfarb is an environmental journalist. His writing has been published in *The Atlantic,* the *New York Times, National Geographic,* and *Orion Magazine* and has been anthologized in the Best American Science and Nature Writing. He is the author of *Crossings: How Road Ecology Is Shaping the Future of Our Planet* and *Eager: The Surprising, Secret Life of Beavers and Why They Matter,* winner of the PEN / E. O. Wilson Literary Science Writing Award.

Annie Hartnett is the author of the novels *Unlikely Animals, Rabbit Cake,* and the forthcoming *The Road to Tender Hearts.* She has been awarded fellowships and residencies from the MacDowell Colony, the Sewanee Writers' Conference, and the Associates of the Boston Public Library. A cohost of the writing and parenting podcast *Good Moms on Paper,* she is a wannabe cartoonist and lives in Massachusetts.

Sean Hill is the author of two poetry collections, *Dangerous Goods,* awarded the Minnesota Book Award in Poetry, and *Blood Ties & Brown Liquor.* Hill has received a fellowship from the Cave Canem Foundation, a Stegner Fellowship from Stanford University, and a Creative Writing Fellowship in Poetry from the National Endowment for the Arts. Hill's poems and essays have been published in *Callaloo, Harvard Review, New England Review, Orion, Oxford American, Poetry,* and *Tin House* as well as in more than two dozen anthologies, including *Black Nature* and *Villanelles.* Hill is director of the Minnesota Northwoods Writers Conference at Bemidji State University and associate professor of creative writing at the University of Montana.

Hester Kaplan is the author of the novels *The Tell* and *Kinship Theory* and the story collections *Unravished* and *The Edge of Marriage,* winner of the Flannery O'Connor Award for Short Fiction. Her fiction and nonfiction have been published in literary journals and anthologies, including *The Best American Short Stories.* She is a cofounder of Goat Hill Writers and is on the faculty of Lesley University's MFA Program in Creative Writing. In 2023 she was named a Mark Twain Fellow for her book *Twice Born: How Mark Twain Helped Me Find My Father.* https:// hesterkaplan.com.

Donika Kelly is author of *The Renunciations,* winner of the Anisfield–Wolf Book Award in poetry, and *Bestiary,* the winner of the 2015 Cave Canem Poetry Prize, a Hurston/Wright Legacy Award, and a Kate Tufts Discovery Award. A recipient of a fellowship from the National Endowment for the Arts, she is a Cave Canem graduate fellow and founding member of the collective Poets at the End of the World.

Christopher Kondrich is a poet, editor, and educator. His most recent book, *Valuing,* is a winner of the National Poetry Series and a *Library Journal* best book of the year. His next book of poetry, *Tread Upon,* is forthcoming from Copper Canyon Press. His poetry and essays are published in *The Believer, The Kenyon Review, Los Angeles Review of Books, The New York Review of Books, The Paris Review,* and *The Yale Review.* He has taught poetry as a visiting assistant professor at the College of the Holy Cross and as a writer-in-residence at the State University of New York at New Paltz. He is a faculty member of Eastern Oregon University's low-residency MFA in Creative and Environmental Writing.

Robin McLean wrote the story collections *Reptile House* and *Get'em Young, Treat'em Tough, Tell'em Nothing.* Her first novel *Pity the Beast* was recognized as a best work of fiction of 2021 in *The Guardian* and *Wall Street Journal.*

Miranda Mellis is the author of *Crocosmia* (forthcoming, Nightboat Books), *The Spokes, The Revisionist, None of This Is Real, Demystifications,* and a number of chapbooks, including most recently *The Revolutionary* and *Unconsciousness Raising.* She has been an artist-in-residence at the Headlands Center for the Arts and Millay Colony and was a recipient of the John Hawkes Prize in Fiction and an NEA grant. She grew up in San Francisco and now lives in the Pacific Northwest where she teaches at Evergreen.

Rajiv Mohabir is the author of four poetry collections, including *Whale Aria, The Taxidermist's Cut,* and *The Cowherd's Son.* His collection

Cutlish was longlisted for the PEN/Voelcker Award for Poetry, a finalist for the New England Book Awards, and a finalist for the 2021 National Book Critics Circle Award. His memoir *Antiman* was a finalist for the Lambda Literary Award in Gay Nonfiction, The Publishing Triangle's Randy Shilts Award for Gay Nonfiction, and the 2022 PEN Open Book Award. He is assistant professor of poetry in the Department of English at the University of Colorado Boulder.

Kyoko Mori is the author of four nonfiction books (*The Dream of Water, Polite Lies, Yarn, Cat and Bird: a Memoir*) and four novels (*Shizuko's Daughter; One Bird; Stone Field, True Arrow; Barn Cat*). Her essays and stories have been published in *The Best American Essays, Harvard Review, The American Scholar, Colorado Review,* and *Conjunctions.* She teaches nonfiction writing in the MFA Program in Creative Writing at George Mason University and the low-residency MFA Program at Lesley University.

David Naimon is the host of the literary podcast *Between the Covers* and coauthor (with Ursula K. Le Guin) of *Ursula K. Le Guin: Conversations on Writing,* winner of the 2019 Locus Award in nonfiction. His writing has been published in *Orion, AGNI, EcoTheo,* and *Boulevard;* cited in *Best American Essays, Best American Travel Writing,* and *Best American Mystery and Suspense;* and reprinted in the Pushcart Prize anthology and *The Best Small Fictions.*

Beth Piatote is a scholar of Native American/Indigenous literature and law; a creative writer of fiction, poetry, plays, and essays; and an Indigenous language revitalization activist, specializing in Nez Perce language and literature. She is the author of two books, *Domestic Subjects: Gender, Citizenship, and Law in Native American Literature* and *The Beadworkers: Stories.* She is Nez Perce, enrolled with the Confederated Tribes of the Colville Reservation.

Rena Priest is an enrolled member of the Lummi Nation. She was Washington State's sixth Poet Laureate (2021–23). She is the editor of a salmon poetry anthology, *I Sing the Salmon Home: Poems from Washington State.* She is the author of two poetry collections and a nonfiction book about beaches. renapriest.com.

Alberto Ríos is the author of fourteen books and chapbooks of poetry, three collections of short stories, a memoir, and a novel. His books of poetry include *Not Go Away Is My Name; A Small Story about the Sky; The Dangerous Shirt; The Theater of Night,* winner of the 2007 PEN/Beyond Margins Award; and *The Smallest Muscle in the Human Body,* a finalist for the National Book Award.

Eléna Rivera is the author of several poetry collections, including *Arrangements, Epic Series, Scaffolding,* and *The Perforated Map.*

Sofia Samatar is a writer of fiction and nonfiction, including the memoir *The White Mosque,* a PEN/Jean Stein Award finalist. Her works range from the award-winning epic fantasy *A Stranger in Olondria* to *Opacities,* a meditation on writing, publishing, and friendship. She teaches African literature, Arabic literature, and speculative fiction at James Madison University in Virginia, where she is Roop Distinguished Professor of English.

Craig Santos Perez is an Indigenous Chamoru (Chamorro) from the Pacific Island of Guåhan (Guam). He is a poet, scholar, editor, publisher, essayist, critic, book reviewer, artist, environmentalist, and political activist. He has written five books of poetry, most recently *Habitat Threshold,* and received the Pen Center USA/Poetry Society of America Literary Prize, the American Book Award, the Lannan Foundation Literary Fellowship, the Hawai'i Literary Arts Council Award for an Established Artist, and a gold medal Nautilus Book Award. He has been a finalist for the *Los Angeles Times* Book Prize and the Kingsley Tufts Award for Poetry, and he was longlisted for a PEN America Literary Award.

Sharma Shields is the author of a short story collection, *Favorite Monster,* and two novels, *The Sasquatch Hunter's Almanac* and *The Cassandra.*

Eleni Sikelianos is the author of ten books of poetry and two hybrid non-fiction histories, including *Your Kingdom, Make Yourself Happy, Body Clock, The Book of Jon, The California Poem, The Monster Lives of Boys & Girls,* and *The Book of Tendons.* Deeply engaged with ecopoetics, her work takes up urgent concerns of environmental precarity and ancestral lineages; her writing is frequently saturated with delight in the natural world and a layperson's study of biology, dedicated to turning the kaleidoscope for more angles on what being alive looks and feels like. https://www.elenisikelianos.com.

Maggie Smith is the *New York Times* bestselling author of seven books of poetry and prose, including *You Could Make This Place Beautiful, Goldenrod, Keep Moving,* and *Good Bones.*

Juliana Spahr is a professor at Mills College at Northeastern University. She is the author most recently of *DuBois's Telegram.* She has written eight volumes of poetry, including *The Winter the Wolf Came, Well Then There Now,* and *Response.* She is the editor with Claudia Rankine of *American Women Poets in the Twenty-first Century.*

Lucy Spelman, executive director and founder of Creature Conserve, is a board-certified zoo and wildlife veterinarian with academic degrees from Brown University and the University of California at Davis. During her tenure as the first woman and youngest person to head the Smithsonian's National Zoo, she brought two giant pandas to the United States from China and launched a ten-year exhibit and facilities renewal project. She worked as a consultant for Animal Planet before moving to central Africa to run the field program for the Gorilla Doctors, which monitors the health of gorillas in Rwanda's Volcanoes National Park and Uganda's Bwindi Impenetrable Forest National Park. She is senior lecturer at the Rhode Island

School of Design, where she teaches biology and conservation to art and design students. She is the author of forty scientific papers, the *National Geographic Animal Encyclopedia,* and *The Rhino with Glue-on Shoes.*

Tim Sutton has degrees in anthropology and communication from the University of Massachusetts Amherst. His writing has been published in the *International Review of Qualitative Research, Qualitative Inquiry,* and *Text and Performance Quarterly.*

Susan Tacent is a writer, scholar, and educator. Her writing has appeared in academic and literary journals, including *Blackbird, DIAGRAM,* and *Tin House Online.* She has taught at various universities, including Brown University, Oberlin College, and Roger Williams University, and has designed and implemented workshops at libraries, arts organizations, and assisted living residences. She is writer-in-residence for Creature Conserve.

Jodie Noel Vinson received an MFA in nonfiction creative writing from Emerson College. Her essays and reviews have been published in *The New York Times, Harvard Review, Literary Hub, Ploughshares, Electric Literature, Agni,* and *Creative Nonfiction.* She received the *Arts & Letters* Susan Atefat Prize for Creative Nonfiction, the *Ninth Letter* Literary Award in Creative Nonfiction, the Maureen Egen Writers Exchange Award from *Poets & Writers,* and a residency from The Jentel Foundation. She is writing a book about the intersections of chronic illness and creative expression.

Asiya Wadud is the author of several poetry collections, most recently *No Knowledge Is Complete Until It Passes Through My Body* and *Mandible Wishbone Solvent.* Her recent writing has been published in *e-flux journal, BOMB Magazine, Triple Canopy, POETRY,* and *Yale Review.* Her work has been supported by the Foundation Jan Michalski, Lower Manhattan Cultural Council, Danspace Project, Finnish Cultural Institute of

New York, Rosendal Theater Norway, and Kunstenfestivaldesarts. Wadud teaches poetry at Saint Ann's School, Columbia University, and Pacific Northwest College of Art.

Claire Wahmanholm is the author of *Meltwater, Redmouth,* and *Wilder.* Her writing has been published in *Sierra, Passages North, The Anarchist Review of Books, The Hopkins Review, Cream City Review, TriQuarterly,* and *The Missouri Review.* She is a 2020–21 McKnight Writing Fellow and the winner of the 2022 Montreal International Poetry Prize.

Marco Wilkinson is the author of *Madder: A Memoir in Weeds.* His essays have been published in *Kenyon Review, Seneca Review, Ecotone,* and *Terrain.* He is assistant professor of literary arts in the Literature Department at the University of California, San Diego.

Jane Wong is the author of the memoir *Meet Me Tonight in Atlantic City* and two books of poetry, *How to Not Be Afraid of Everything* and *Overpour.*

Creature Conserve

Growing Art–Sci Pathways for Wildlife Conservation

The mission of Creature Conserve, a Rhode Island–based nonprofit, is to grow a creative community that combines art with science to cultivate new pathways for wildlife conservation. The organization brings together artists, designers, writers, scientists, traditional knowledge holders, and other experts in a supportive, welcoming space to learn about threats to wildlife, share empathy for animals, exchange ideas, and find opportunities for growth at the intersection of art, science, and conservation. Programs include curatorial programs, mentorship, scholarships, and workshops. Participants from all countries learn from each other, create and innovate together, develop new skills, and use their combined talents to reach a wider audience and improve wildlife conservation outcomes.